AMERICA IS UNDER CYBER ATTACK: WHY URGENT ACTION IS NEEDED

HEARING

BEFORE THE

SUBCOMMITTEE ON OVERSIGHT, INVESTIGATIONS, AND MANAGEMENT

OF THE

COMMITTEE ON HOMELAND SECURITY

HOUSE OF REPRESENTATIVES

ONE HUNDRED TWELFTH CONGRESS

SECOND SESSION

APRIL 24, 2012

Serial No. 112–85

Printed for the use of the Committee on Homeland Security

Available via the World Wide Web: http://www.gpo.gov/fdsys/

U.S. GOVERNMENT PRINTING OFFICE

77–380 PDF   WASHINGTON : 2013

For sale by the Superintendent of Documents, U.S. Government Printing Office
Internet: bookstore.gpo.gov Phone: toll free (866) 512–1800; DC area (202) 512–1800
Fax: (202) 512–2250   Mail: Stop SSOP, Washington, DC 20402–0001

COMMITTEE ON HOMELAND SECURITY

PETER T. KING, New York, *Chairman*

LAMAR SMITH, Texas
DANIEL E. LUNGREN, California
MIKE ROGERS, Alabama
MICHAEL T. MCCAUL, Texas
GUS M. BILIRAKIS, Florida
PAUL C. BROUN, Georgia
CANDICE S. MILLER, Michigan
TIM WALBERG, Michigan
CHIP CRAVAACK, Minnesota
JOE WALSH, Illinois
PATRICK MEEHAN, Pennsylvania
BEN QUAYLE, Arizona
SCOTT RIGELL, Virginia
BILLY LONG, Missouri
JEFF DUNCAN, South Carolina
TOM MARINO, Pennsylvania
BLAKE FARENTHOLD, Texas
ROBERT L. TURNER, New York

BENNIE G. THOMPSON, Mississippi
LORETTA SANCHEZ, California
SHEILA JACKSON LEE, Texas
HENRY CUELLAR, Texas
YVETTE D. CLARKE, New York
LAURA RICHARDSON, California
DANNY K. DAVIS, Illinois
BRIAN HIGGINS, New York
CEDRIC L. RICHMOND, Louisiana
HANSEN CLARKE, Michigan
WILLIAM R. KEATING, Massachusetts
KATHLEEN C. HOCHUL, New York
JANICE HAHN, California
RON BARBER, Arizona

MICHAEL J. RUSSELL, *Staff Director/Chief Counsel*
KERRY ANN WATKINS, *Senior Policy Director*
MICHAEL S. TWINCHEK, *Chief Clerk*
I. LANIER AVANT, *Minority Staff Director*

———

SUBCOMMITTEE ON OVERSIGHT, INVESTIGATIONS, AND MANAGEMENT

MICHAEL T. MCCAUL, Texas, *Chairman*

GUS M. BILIRAKIS, Florida
BILLY LONG, Missouri, *Vice Chair*
JEFF DUNCAN, South Carolina
TOM MARINO, Pennsylvania
PETER T. KING, New York *(Ex Officio)*

WILLIAM R. KEATING, Massachusetts
YVETTE D. CLARKE, New York
DANNY K. DAVIS, Illinois
BENNIE G. THOMPSON, Mississippi *(Ex Officio)*

DR. R. NICK PALARINO, *Staff Director*
DIANA BERGWIN, *Subcommittee Clerk*
TAMLA SCOTT, *Minority Subcommittee Director*

CONTENTS

AMERICA IS UNDER CYBER ATTACK: WHY URGENT ACTION IS NEEDED

Tuesday, April 24, 2012

U.S. HOUSE OF REPRESENTATIVES,
SUBCOMMITTEE ON OVERSIGHT, INVESTIGATIONS, AND
MANAGEMENT,
COMMITTEE ON HOMELAND SECURITY,
Washington, DC.

The subcommittee met, pursuant to call, at 2:05 p.m., in Room 311, Cannon House Office Building, Hon. Michael T. McCaul [Chairman of the subcommittee] presiding.

Present: Representatives McCaul, Long, Duncan, Keating, Clarke, Davis, and Thompson (ex officio).

Mr. MCCAUL. The committee will come to order. The purpose of our hearing is to examine the evolving computer hacking threats from nation-states and hacker groups to Government, financial institutions, American businesses, and personal computer networks.

I now recognize myself for an opening statement. America's computers are under attack and every American is at risk. The United States Government, critical infrastructures, American business institutions, and our personal data are being compromised by nation-states and hacker groups. Their intent is to conduct cyber warfare, paralyzing our infrastructure, stealing our intellectual property, conducting espionage, and gaining access to our credit card, bank account, and Social Security numbers.

Richard Clarke, Former Special Advisor on Cybersecurity to President Bush, said within the first 48 hours of a cyber attack on the United States we could experience the Department of Defense's classified and unclassified networks collapsing as a result of large-scale routers failing to function, reports of large oil refinery fires as well as lethal clouds of chlorine gas emitting from chemical plants, our financial system dissolving as a result of important financial data being lost with no idea of who owns what, pipelines carrying natural gas exploding, trains and subways derailed, a Nation-wide blackout leaving American cities in the dark.

Unfortunately, this is not a science fiction scenario. There are no shells exploding or foreign militaries on our shores. But make no mistake: America is under attack by digital bombs. There are several things the American public should understand about these attacks. They are real, stealthy, and persistent, and could devastate our Nation. They occur at the speed of light. They are global and can come from anywhere on the Earth. They penetrate traditional defenses.

So who is conducting these attacks and why? An October 2011 report to Congress on foreign economic collection and industrial espionage states, it is part of China and Russia's national policy to try to identify and steal sensitive technology which they need for their development. China and Russia view themselves as strategic competitors of the United States and are the most aggressive collectors of U.S. economic information and technology. China's cyber warfare capabilities and the espionage campaigns they have undertaken are the most prevalent of any nation-state actor. China has created citizen hacker groups, engaged in cyber espionage, established cyber war military units and laced the infrastructure with logic bombs.

Russia has advanced capabilities and the intent and technological prowess necessary to carry out a cyber attack anywhere in the world at any time. Russia has been accused of unleashing a cyber war against Estonia in 2011 and shutting down government websites. Russia has also taken down Georgia's banking and government sites as part of a policy to demonstrate its power during a conflict.

There are, of course, many other countries developing cyber capabilities and using cyber espionage to steal U.S. trade and technology secrets to bolster their own economic development, and all of them pose a threat. Besides nation-states, there are groups such as Anonymous, Moltsec, and AntiSec who indulge in non-state hacktivism or hacking and activism. They are largely a sympathizer for freedom of information and their agenda is basically to protest what they perceive as violations of privacy. These attacks are sometimes aimed at individuals but many times used against businesses.

Based on recent arrests here in the United Kingdom—here and in the United Kingdom—it appears that the groups consist predominantly of juveniles who want notoriety. Non-state hacktivist groups have indulged in denial of service attacks against the likes of Sony, MasterCard, and Stratfor located in my hometown of Austin, Texas. They deface websites, slow down on-line access to the internet and steal sensitive information such as password files, credit card information, and Social Security numbers. These groups, both nation-states and non-state hacktivists, present a threat not only to the security of our Nation but also to our personal and business files.

We require a robust National effort to counter these attacks against our National interest. The potential of cyber attacks is frightening. The Stuxnet worm is groundbreaking malware launched against the uranium nuclear program. It was used to blow up centrifuges. It is so devious in its use of computer vulnerabilities, with such a multi-pronged approach, that the Iranians had no idea they were being attacked. Such a successful attack against the United States, with viruses designed to manipulate and bring down our industrial control systems, could cause devastating human and economic losses.

Indeed, General Alexander, Director of the National Security Agency, told me that it is not a matter of "if" but "when" a cyber Pearl Harbor will occur. We have been fortunate that up until this point, cyber attacks in our country have not caused a cataclysmic event that has brought physical harm to Americans, but that is not for lack of an effort on the part of those who mean to destroy our way of life.

Last week Former Secretary of Homeland Security Michael Chertoff said it doesn't take a lot to understand how an attack on critical infrastructure during a time of tension could seriously undermine the ability of a country to defend itself. The Secretary recalled: "I had the experience of living through an event that occurred after there was a fair amount of warning, and four planes were hijacked and we lost about 3,000 people. My message to anybody who is interested in this, particularly in the Congress, is let's do something meaningful because it is not a tolerable situation."

I share the Secretary's concerns. It is time to do something meaningful.

[The statement of Mr. McCaul follows:]

STATEMENT OF CHAIRMAN MICHAEL T. MCCAUL

APRIL 24, 2012

America's computers are under attack and every American is at risk. The U.S. Government, critical infrastructures, American business institutions, and our personal data are being compromised by nation-states and hacker groups.

The intent is to conduct cyber warfare, paralyzing our infrastructure, stealing our intellectual property, conducting espionage, and gaining access to our credit card, bank account, and Social Security numbers.

Richard Clarke, former special adviser on cybersecurity to President George W. Bush, said within the first 48 hours of a cyber attack on the United States we could experience:

• The Department of Defense's classified and unclassified networks collapsing as a result of large-scale routers failing to function.
• Reports of large oil refinery fires, as well as lethal clouds of chlorine gas emitting from chemical plants.
• Our financial system dissolving as a result of important financial data being lost with no idea of who owns what.
• Pipelines carrying natural gas exploding.
• Trains and subway derailing.
• A Nation-wide blackout leaving American cities in the dark.

Unfortunately, this is not a science fiction scenario.

There are no shells exploding or foreign militaries on our shores. But make no mistake: America is under attack by digital bombs.

There are several things the American public should understand about these attacks:

• They are real, stealthy, and persistent, and could devastate our Nation.
• They occur at the speed of light.
• They are global and could come from anywhere on earth.
• They penetrate traditional defenses.

Who is conducting these attacks and why?

An October 2011 Report to Congress on Foreign Economic Collection and Industrial Espionage states, it is part of China and Russia's national policy to try to identify and steal sensitive technology, which they need for their development. China and Russia view themselves as strategic competitors of the United States and are the most aggressive collectors of U.S. economic information and technology.

China's cyber warfare capabilities and the espionage campaigns they have undertaken are the most prevalent of any nation-state actor. China has created citizen hacker groups, engaged in cyber espionage, established cyber war military units, and laced the U.S. infrastructure with logic bombs.

Russia has advanced capabilities and the intent and technological prowess necessary to carry out a cyber attack anywhere in the world, at any time.

Russia has been accused of unleashing a cyber war against Estonia in 2007 and shutting down government websites.

Russia has also taken down Georgia's banking and government sites as part of a policy to demonstrate its power during a conflict.

There are of course many other countries developing cyber capabilities and using cyber espionage to steal U.S. trade and technology secrets to bolster their own economic development; and all of them pose a threat. Besides nation-states, there are groups such as Anonymous, LulzSec and AntiSec who indulge in non-state "hacktivism" or hacking and activism.

They are largely a sympathizer for "freedom of information," and their agenda is basically to protest what they perceive as violations of privacy.

These attacks are sometimes aimed at individuals but many times used against businesses.

Based on the recent arrests here and in the United Kingdom, it appears the groups consist predominantly of juveniles who want notoriety.

Non-state hacktivist groups have indulged in denial of service attacks against the likes of Sony, Mastercard, and Stratfor, located in my hometown of Austin, Texas, defacing websites, slowing down on-line accesses on the internet and stealing sensitive information such as password files, credit card, and Social Security numbers.

These groups, both nation-states and non-state hacktivists, present a threat not only to the security of our Nation, but also to our personal and business files. We require a robust National effort to counter these attacks against our National interests.

The potential of cyber attacks is frightening. The Stuxnet worm is groundbreaking malware launched against the Iranian nuclear program. It is so devious in its use of computer vulnerabilities with such a multipronged approach that the Iranians had no idea they were attacked.

Such a successful attack against the United States with viruses designed to manipulate and bring down our industrial control systems they could cause devastating human and economic losses.

General Alexander, director of the National Security Agency, told me that it is not a matter of if, but when a cyber Pearl Harbor will occur.

We have been fortunate that up until this point cyber attacks in our country have not caused a cataclysmic event that has brought physical harm to Americans. But that is not for lack of effort on the part of those who mean to destroy our way of life.

Last week, former Secretary of Homeland Security Michael Chertoff said "It doesn't take a lot to understand how an attack on critical infrastructure during a time of tension could seriously undermine the ability of a country to defend itself."

The Secretary recalled, "I had the experience of living through an event that occurred after there was a fair amount of warning and four planes were hijacked and we lost about 3,000 people. My message to anybody who's interested in this, particularly in Congress, is let's do something meaningful because it is not a tolerable situation."

I share the Secretary's concerns. It is time to do something meaningful.

Mr. McCAUL. With that, I recognize the Ranking Member of the subcommittee, Mr. Keating, for his opening statement.

Mr. KEATING. Thank you, Mr. Chairman. Mr. Chairman, thank you for convening today's hearing. I would also like to acknowledge Chairman McCaul's long-standing interest in cybersecurity efforts. I want to also acknowledge the presence of Ms. Clarke, who is the Ranking Subcommittee Chair on Cybersecurity, as well as Ranking Member Thompson, whose interest in this issue has been long-standing, and he is the Ranking Member of the overall committee.

In 2007 Chairman McCaul, along with Congressman Jim Langevin, were named co-chairs of the Center for Strategic and International Studies Commission on Cybersecurity for the 44th Presidency. Since that time he, among others, have been leaders on this issue, and last month he and I co-hosted a House-wide cybersecurity briefing that included an in-depth discussion on how cyber attacks threaten our critical infrastructure, cell phones, and computers.

I am pleased to see that two of the participating organizations in that briefing—CSIS, the Center for Strategic and International Studies, and Northeastern University—are testifying today. I look forward to continuing to work with Chairman McCaul on cybersecurity issues and performing oversight of the Department's role as a leading cybersecurity agency.

Cybersecurity, as acknowledged by President Obama, is one of the most serious economic and National security threats our Nation faces. The impacts of a cyber attack against critical infrastructure or our widely-used Federal system are spurring efforts in Washington to compel energy companies, along with other operators of vital infrastructures, to do more to protect their computer network from hackers. Public reports reveal Federal networks have been under attack for years, and some accounts point to upwards to 3 billion cyber attacks a year in the United States. The price of the security is not cheap. Government agencies would need to boost cybersecurity spending more than seven times to block 95 percent of hacker attacks, according to a Bloomberg Government study.

That translates into an annual spending average of $190.3 million per agency, up from the current $26 million, according to the study based on interviews with officials of 48 Federal, State, and municipal agencies.

Moreover, one recent study estimated that 71 percent of all companies experienced a cyber attack last year. The current combined financial impact on public and private sector cyber attacks is unknown, but estimates are in the billions. Yet as we add up the dollars and weigh the risks, we must not forget the greatest attack will be on the confidence of the American people if even one large-scale cyber attack scenario were to materialize.

It is therefore imperative that we get a full understanding of the root causes of cyber attacks, learn from where the threat is derived, and ensure that every available means of protection is deployed at our disposal.

Mr. Chairman, last week during our full committee's markup of the Precise Act, I proposed an amendment that would have incorporated the model of the three-legged stool of Government working in partnership with academia and industry and to legislation designed to anticipate cyber threats and develop means to combat them.

I plan to work further in this initiative because even in times of greatly-needed cost-saving measures, we should be wary of trading in long-term gains for short-term cuts. For this reason, our Government should do more to accelerate the pace of research discovery and development in home-grown technologies. I believe that this path forward will enable us to see a return on our investments and remain competitive in the global economy as well.

I know that my colleague, Chairman McCaul, is a proponent of engaging research institutions in these matters, and I congratulate him and his work on the Cybersecurity Enhancement Act of 2011. Unfortunately, this week the House will consider legislation that contains broad and ambiguous language, serious privacy implications, and that moves away from Homeland Security being the central agency for cybersecurity efforts.

The Department through its United States Computer Emergency Readiness Team, or US–CERT, has made great strides, and I am concerned that the legislation compromising its authority will set us back in our fight against cyber attacks. The President, the CSIS Commission on Cybersecurity for the 44th Presidency, and the

House Republican Cybersecurity Task Force have all made numerous recommendations on how to improve cybersecurity. I would encourage my colleagues to bring legislation to the floor that fully protects the Constitutional rights and contains recommendations made by these entities.

I look forward to today's testimony and am especially glad to hear from Dr. Stephen Flynn of Northeastern University as he discusses the nature of the cybersecurity threat and his standpoint on making universities full-fledged cybersecurity partners. I yield back.

Mr. MCCAUL. I thank the Ranking Member, and thank you for your special recognition of our efforts and my efforts as well.

With that, I recognize the Ranking Member of the full committee, Mr. Thompson.

Mr. THOMPSON. Thank you very much, Chairman McCaul, for today's hearing. The threat to our Nation's cyber systems and networks is real and present. Billions of Americans use the internet every day to communicate, pay bills, obtain information, and perform job-related functions. Moreover, the Federal Government relies on the internet and a network of Federal systems to support infrastructure, maintain defense systems, protect power plants and water supplies, perform administrative functions of Federal agencies, and a host of other activities.

It is therefore imperative that we take seriously the United States' role in securing cyber space from unwanted intrusions and dangerous attacks. A large portion of Federal responsibility lies with the U.S. Congress. It is our role to ensure that necessary legislation is passed and provide America with the protection it needs. Per the title of today's hearing, urgent action is needed, and I agree.

However I have consistently noted that what is needed is legislation that will accomplish three things: No. 1, address the growing cyber threat to critical infrastructure networks; No. 2, promote and enhance information sharing between and among private sector and the Federal Government while protecting the privacy and civil liberties of Americans using the internet; and No. 3, solidify and enhance the Department of Homeland Security's role as a Federal Government lead for Federal network security and private sector cyber support.

Unfortunately, none of the bills being voted on by the House this week accomplish these goals. As a result, at the end of Cybersecurity Week, America will remain without a comprehensive National strategy that bears cybersecurity efforts in one domestic agency and protects the privacy rights of American citizens.

While the initial measure introduced by Representative Lungren, the chairman of the Committee's Subcommittee on Cybersecurity, Infrastructure Protection, and Security Technologies was not perfect, it took a number of steps in the right direction and would have measurably strengthened our Nation's cybersecurity posture. Yet the key initiatives that I believe were necessary were removed at the last minute. Despite these changes, the Republican leadership has elected not to bring that measure to the House floor.

So while I look forward to today's testimony and thank the witnesses for their participation, I am disheartened by the missed opportunity to produce the urgent action that is indeed needed. I yield back, Mr. Chairman.

Mr. McCAUL. I thank the Ranking Member. I share your concerns. I do want to say that there are four bills that will be on the House floor this week, all of which passed out of committee in a bipartisan fashion. I believe it is the leadership's intent to proceed with those bills that will go forward in a bipartisan way, as this is an issue that should be a bipartisan issue and not a partisan issue. Unfortunately, the bill passed out of Homeland Security was not a bipartisan vote.

When I talked to Secretary of Homeland Security Napolitano and General Alexander, the NSA director, the two key components they wanted to see was a codification of the existing legal authorities based on Presidential Directives and Executive Orders. The bill passed out of committee does that. Also with respect to information sharing, that is achieved through the National Cybersecurity and Communications Integration Center. So I think those two key components are addressed in the bill.

But let me just say this to the Ranking Member. I hope that we can work together to make this bill out of this important committee, with the agency that really is in the forefront and the center of cybersecurity. I hope we can work together to make this a more bipartisan bill and proceed to the House floor.

With that, other Members are reminded that opening statements may be submitted for the record. We are pleased to have a very distinguished panel here before us today.

First, Mr. Henry needs probably little or no introduction and I can't tell you how pleased I am to have him here today. He has been a real leader in this area. He is a former executive assistant director of the Criminal, Cyber, Response, and Services Branch of the FBI, really at the forefront of this effort for so many years. He was responsible for all FBI world-wide computer investigations. Additionally, he was an original member of the National cyber study group which developed a comprehensive National Cybersecurity Initiative.

Next we have a dear friend of mine, a colleague, somebody I worked with, as the Ranking Member mentioned, on the CSIS Commission report on cybersecurity, Dr. James Lewis. Jim is a senior fellow and director of the Technology and Public Policy Program at the Center for Strategic and International Studies focusing on technology, National security and the international economy. Previously he was the project director for the CSIS Commission on Cybersecurity for the 44th Presidency. Jim, great to see you here again today.

Next we have Mr. Gregory Wilshusen. It is hard to say that three times in a row and get it right. But Greg is the director of information security issues at the GAO where he leads information security-related studies and audits of the Federal Government. Thank you for being here as well.

Next we have Mr. Stuart McClure who is the executive vice president and the worldwide chief technology officer at McAfee. Most of you know McAfee is a leader in cybersecurity efforts. At McAfee he also served as senior vice president of global threats and research.

Finally we have Dr. Flynn. Dr. Stephen Flynn is the founding co-director of the George Kostas Research Institute for Homeland Security at Northeastern University. Prior to September 11 he served as an expert advisor to the U.S. Commission on National Security, the Hart-Rudman Commission. Dr. Flynn served in the Coast Guard on active duty for 20 years, and we thank you for your service, Dr. Flynn, in that regard.

So with that, the Chairman now recognizes Mr. Henry for his testimony.

STATEMENT OF SHAWN HENRY, FORMER EXECUTIVE ASSISTANT DIRECTOR, CRIMINAL, CYBER, RESPONSE, AND SERVICES BRANCH, FEDERAL BUREAU OF INVESTIGATION

Mr. HENRY. Good afternoon Chairman McCaul, Ranking Member Keating, and Members of the subcommittee. I am pleased to be here today with the distinguished witnesses to discuss the cyber threats facing our Nation and how these threats impact our Government and our private-sector networks. It is difficult to overstate the potential harm these threats pose to our economy, our National security, and the critical infrastructure upon which our country relies.

I am currently the president of CrowdStrike Services, a computer security organization. But up until last month I led all the FBI cyber efforts, as the Chairman noted, and I saw with deep granularity the threats that we face. The number and sophistication of these cyber attacks has increased dramatically over the past 5 years and it is going to continue to grow. The threat has reached the point that given enough time, motivation, and funding, a determined adversary will likely penetrate any system that is accessible directly from the network. I do not believe our critical infrastructure can remain unscathed in the long term if the current environment remains unchanged. With the depth and breadth of the intrusions that I have seen, I believe it is necessary for network administrators to assume that they have already been breached rather than waiting for their network intrusion systems to alert them to an infiltration.

Network security compliance in and of itself falls far short of the continuous evaluation that needs to be done on our networks every single day. Cyber criminal threats to the United States result in significant economic losses. Cyber criminals are forming private trusted and organized groups to conduct cyber crime, and these groups are accessing personally identifiable information which includes banking, brokerage account information, credentials and credit card numbers of individuals and businesses that can be used for financial gain. The economic consequences are severe, and there have been hundreds of millions of dollars lost in the financial services sector alone.

But that doesn't even begin to tell the real story about what is happening to this Nation. A colleague of mine recently used an analogy where an iceberg represents the totality of threats to the information infrastructure. Cyber crime, as I have just described, is merely the tip of the iceberg. The biggest threats are below the waterline, just like the vast majority of an iceberg. The public sees the tip because cyber crime is regularly reported in the media—

stolen credit cards, lost identities, eastern European organized crime groups, and breached bank accounts. The waterline is the separation between the unclassified and classified environment. Thus, the most sophisticated and damaging attacks occur primarily out of the public sight.

I would offer that only a small percentage of individuals, primarily those in the intelligence community, have ever seen below the waterline, and the real threat is grossly underappreciated by the public.

The most significant cyber threats to our Nation are those with high intent and high capability to inflict damage or even death in the United States, to illicitly acquire substantial assets, or to illegally obtain sensitive or unclassified U.S. military, intelligence, or economic information. These are the threats from foreign intelligence services who assault U.S. businesses many times every single day, 365, and for those I have seen below the waterline.

The threat continues unabated. U.S. critical infrastructure faces a growing threat due to advancements in the availability and sophistication of malicious software tools and the fact that new technologies raise new security issues that are not always addressed prior to adoption. Specifically, industrial control systems which operate the physical processes of the Nation's pipelines, electricity, and other critical infrastructures are at elevated risk of cyber exploitation.

Today, likely only advanced threat actors are capable of employing these techniques. But as we have seen with other malicious software tools, these capabilities will eventually be within reach of all threat actors.

So what does this all mean? I believe most major companies have already been breached or will be breached, resulting in substantial losses of information, economic competitiveness, and National security. Many are breached and have absolutely no knowledge that an adversary was or remains resident on their network, oftentimes for weeks, months, or even years.

While I was executive assistant director at the FBI, our agents regularly knocked on the door of victim companies and told them their network had been intruded upon and their corporate secrets had been stolen because we found their proprietary data resident on a server in the course of another investigation. We were routinely telling organizations they were victims, and these victims ranged in size and industry and cut across all financial critical sectors, or all critical sectors.

For those companies that do know and fail to report or address the breach, they are aiding and assisting in the foreign intelligence service collection, and their corporate infrastructure is a component of the adversary's collection platform. Although our adversary cyber capabilities are at an all-time high, combating this challenge needs to be a top priority for both the public and the private sector.

The adversary is persistent. It is not enough to stop their attack once or twice. They will keep coming until they get in. The problem with existing technologies and threat mitigation tactics is they are too focused on adversary tools like malware and exploits, and not on who the adversary is and how they operate.

Ultimately, we focus on the enemy and take the fight to them to raise their cost of attack, and we will fail because they will always get through if we don't take that approach. This requires us to stop solely playing defense. The sophisticated adversary practices crafty offense and the offense outpaces the defense. While we certainly need to continue defense and not let our guard down, we need to be more proactive and strategic in our approach. We cannot stand by and wait for them to trip an alarm as they shake the proverbial fence, because the sophisticated adversaries are jumping right over the fence. They are never tripping an alarm. They are bypassing the intrusion detection systems. We must assume that they are already inside the perimeter and we must constantly hunt them on our networks to identify and mitigate their actions.

Hunting necessitates us acquiring a better sight picture of who the adversary is, the assets they are targeting, the techniques they are employing and who exactly they are. This is where intelligence sharing is critical.

Technology is just a piece of the solution, not the sole solution. What we have is an adversary problem, not a malware problem. Let me repeat that piece about intelligence. The sharing of intelligence is critical and the U.S. Government needs to develop better protocols to share intelligence broadly across the private sector.

In conclusion, we face significant challenges in our efforts to combat the cyber attack. I am optimistic that by strengthening partnerships and effectively sharing intelligence and successfully identifying our adversaries, we can best protect our businesses and critical infrastructure. However, I would be remiss if I didn't say this: Recognizing this is a complex problem; there are many moving parts. I appreciate the committee's statement about the sense of urgency. It is really, really important because our Nation is at risk and we cannot stand by and admire this problem.

I look forward to working with the subcommittee and Congress as a whole to determine a successful course forward and ensure that we can have a safe, positive, economic, and social benefit from the internet while minimizing the risks posed to us by our adversaries.

[The prepared statement of Mr. Henry follows:]

PREPARED STATEMENT OF SHAWN HENRY

APRIL 24, 2012

Good afternoon Chairman McCaul, Ranking Member Keating, and Members of the subcommittee. I'm pleased to be here today to discuss the cyber threats facing our Nation and how these threats impact our Government and private-sector networks. It is difficult to overstate the potential harm these threats pose to our economy, our National security, and the critical infrastructure upon which our country relies.

THE CYBERSECURITY THREAT

As the subcommittee is aware, the number and sophistication of cyber attacks has increased dramatically over the past 5 years and is expected to continue to grow. The threat has reached the point that, given enough time, motivation, and funding, a determined adversary will likely penetrate any system that is accessible directly from the internet. Even systems not touching the network are susceptible to attack via other than remote access, including the trusted insider using devices such as USB flash drives, and the supply chain.

It is difficult to say with confidence that our critical infrastructure—the backbone of our country's economic prosperity, National security, and public health—will remain unscathed and always be available when needed. In fact, I have stated publicly that with the depth and breadth of the intrusions I've seen, I believe it is necessary for network administrators to assume they have already been breached rather than waiting for their intrusion detection systems to alert them to an infiltration.

CRIMINAL CYBER THREATS AGAINST THE PRIVATE SECTOR

Cyber criminal threats to the United States result in significant economic losses. Cyber criminals are forming private, trusted, and organized groups to conduct cyber crime. The adoption of specialized skill sets and professionalized business practices by these criminals is steadily increasing the complexity of cyber crime by providing actors of all technical abilities with the necessary tools and resources to conduct cyber crime. Not only are criminals advancing their abilities to attack a system remotely, they are becoming adept at tricking victims into compromising their own systems.

Once a system is compromised, cyber criminals will use their accesses to obtain Personally Identifiable Information (PII), which includes on-line banking/brokerage account credentials and credit card numbers of individuals and businesses that can be used for financial gain. As cyber crime groups increasingly recruit experienced actors and pool resources and knowledge, they advance their ability to be successful in crimes against more profitable targets and will learn the skills necessary to evade the security industry and law enforcement.

The potential economic consequences are severe. The sting of a cyber crime is not felt equally across the board. A small company may not be able to survive even one significant cyber attack.

Often, businesses are unable to recoup their losses, and it may be impossible to estimate their damage. Many companies prefer not to disclose that their systems have been compromised, so they absorb the loss, making it impossible to accurately calculate damages. As a result of the inability to define and calculate losses, the best that the Government and private sector can offer are estimates. Over the past 5 years, estimates of the costs of cyber crime to the U.S. economy have ranged from millions to hundreds of billions. A 2010 study conducted by the Ponemon Institute estimated that the median annual cost of cyber crime to an individual victim organization ranges from $1 million to $52 million.

According to a 2011 publication released by Javelin Strategy and Research, the annual cost of identity theft is $37 billion. This includes all forms of identity theft, not just cyber means. The Internet Crime Complaint Center (IC3), which aggregates self-reported complaints of cyber crime, reports that in 2010, identity theft schemes made up 9.8 percent of all cyber crime.

THE TIP OF THE ICEBERG

A colleague of mine recently used an analogy where an iceberg represents the totality of threats to the information infrastructure. "Cyber crime", as described above, is merely the tip of the iceberg; the biggest threats are "below the water line", just like the vast majority of an iceberg. The public sees "the tip" because the cyber "crime" is regularly reported in the media; stolen credit cards, lost identities, Eastern European Organized Crime groups; and breached bank accounts. The "water line" is the separation between the unclassified and classified environment; thus, the most sophisticated and damaging attacks occur primarily out of the public's sight.

I would offer that only a very small group of individuals—primarily those in the intelligence community—have ever seen "below the water line", and the real threat is grossly underappreciated by the public. The most significant cyber threats to our Nation are those with high intent and high capability to inflict damage or even death in the United States; to illicitly acquire substantial assets; or to illegally obtain sensitive or classified U.S. military, intelligence, or economic information. These are the threats from foreign intelligence services, and for those I have seen below the waterline.

CYBER THREATS TO U.S. CRITICAL INFRASTRUCTURE

The threat continues unabated. U.S. critical infrastructure faces a growing cyber threat due to advancements in the availability and sophistication of malicious software tools and the fact that new technologies raise new security issues that are not always addressed prior to adoption. The increasing automation of our infrastructures provides more cyber access points for adversaries to exploit, and the target set grows daily as more and more data is pushed, transmitted, or stored on the network.

New "smart grid" and "smart home" products, for example, designed to provide remote communication and control of devices in our residences, businesses, and critical infrastructures, must be developed and implemented in ways that will also provide protection from unauthorized use. Otherwise, each new device will become a doorway into our systems for adversaries to use for their own purposes.

Industrial control systems, which operate the physical processes of the Nation's pipelines, railroads, and other critical infrastructures, are at elevated risk of cyber exploitation. We need to be concerned about the proliferation of malicious techniques that could degrade, disrupt, or destroy critical infrastructure. Though likely only advanced threat actors are currently capable of employing these techniques, as we have seen with other malicious software tools, these capabilities will eventually be within reach of all threat actors.

WHAT DOES ALL THIS MEAN?

I believe most major companies have already been breached or will be breached, resulting in substantial losses of information, economic competitiveness, and National security. Many are breached and have absolutely no knowledge that an adversary was or remains resident on their network, often times for weeks, months, or even years. While I was EAD at the FBI, our agents regularly knocked on the door of victim companies and told them their network had been intruded upon and their corporate secrets stolen, because we found their proprietary data resident on a server in the course of another investigation. We were routinely telling organizations they were victims, and these victims ranged in size and industry, and cut across all critical sectors.

ADDRESSING THE THREAT

Although our cyber adversaries' capabilities are at an all-time high, combating this challenge needs to be a top priority for both the public and the private sector. We need to continue to develop partnerships within industry, academia, and across all of Government to have a dramatic improvement in our ability to share intelligence to combat this threat.

The adversary is persistent. It's not enough to stop their attack once or twice; they will keep trying until they get in. The problem with existing technologies and threat-mitigation tactics is they are too focused on adversary tools (malware and exploits) and not on who the adversary is and how they operate. Ultimately, until we focus on the enemy and take the fight to them to raise their cost of attack, we will fail because they will always get thorough.

This requires us to stop relying solely on "defense." The sophisticated adversary practices crafty offense, and the offense outpaces the defense. While we certainly need to continue defense—we cannot let our guard down—we need to be more proactive and strategic in our approach.

We cannot stand by and wait for them to trip an alarm as they shake the proverbial fence; sophisticated adversaries jump OVER the fence, bypassing the intrusion detection "alarm" entirely. We must assume they are already inside the perimeter, and we must constantly hunt them on our networks to identify and mitigate their actions.

Hunting necessitates us acquiring a better site picture of the adversary—what assets are they targeting, what techniques are they employing, and who, exactly, are they? This is where intelligence sharing is critical; using advanced intelligence technology, companies can share information enabling them to learn the human aspects of the attack, become more predictive, and thus preventative. Technology is a piece of the solution, not the sole solution, because what we really have is an adversary problem.

CONCLUSION

We face significant challenges in our efforts to combat the cyber threat. I am optimistic that by strengthening partnerships, effectively sharing intelligence, and successfully identifying our adversaries, we can best protect businesses and critical infrastructure from grave damage.

I look forward to assisting the subcommittee and Congress as a whole to determine a successful course forward for the Nation that allows us to reap the positive economic and social benefits of the internet while minimizing the risk posed by those who seek to use it to do us irreparable harm.

Mr. McCAUL. Thank you Mr. Henry for your service and for your insight to this committee.

Next, the Chairman recognizes Mr. Lewis.

STATEMENT OF JAMES A. LEWIS, DIRECTOR AND SENIOR FELLOW, TECHNOLOGY AND PUBLIC POLICY PROGRAM, CENTER FOR STRATEGIC AND INTERNATIONAL STUDIES

Mr. LEWIS. Thank you, Mr. Chairman. Thanks to the Members of the committee for the opportunity to testify. Many of you, of course, are already familiar with the problem, so I will touch on two issues in particular: Cyber espionage and cyber attack. Cyber espionage is our biggest problem, as you just heard, but most breaches are not reported. The best example is the 2010 Google incident which involved at least 35 other Fortune 500 companies, none of whom reported a problem. Concealing losses makes business sense, but it also makes it hard to plan a good defense. Perhaps the new SEC ruling will change this, but it hasn't changed yet.

It is difficult to value the loss from cyber espionage, but all the estimates I have looked at put it in the tens or even hundreds of billions of dollars per year. The damage from espionage depends on whether the acquiring nation can use the technology. Sometimes it can take years for them to benefit. In other cases the benefit can be immediate, and we can identify foreign programs that appear to be based on U.S. technology. The clearest damage comes from the loss of military technology, but America's technological leadership and economic competitiveness is at risk. The fastest growing threat comes from the proliferation of the ability to attack critical infrastructure.

We have been hearing about cyber Pearl Harbors and cyber Armageddons for about 15 years, and a reasonable person could ask: Why isn't this hype? Here is why it is not hype. Experiments at Idaho National Labs in 2007 showed that software sent over the internet could cause physical destruction by exploiting vulnerabilities in industrial control systems. Stuxnet confirmed this. There has been at least one other unreported incident. Just yesterday we saw oil facilities in Iran damaged by cyber attack.

Only a few countries currently have this capability but new classes of opponents want them and are seeking to acquire them. This includes Iran and North Korea. These regimes are not known for stable decision making. Both have development programs and both have experimented with attacks. FBI Director Mueller points out that Iran may be losing its reluctance to attack the United States directly.

Non-state actors, particularly Western anti-Government groups, are also exploring cyber attack. You can download the tools that will find critical infrastructure vulnerabilities easily off the internet. I did it last week and I toyed around with it and found 6,000 vulnerable networks. It was kind of fun. Combine these reconnaissance tools with the attack tools available in the cyber crime black market, and someone with good hacking skills—and there are many in these groups—could attack the poorly-defended critical infrastructures that are found in this country.

As cyber attack capabilities become commoditized, the temptation for these politically motivated groups to use them against vulnerable U.S. targets will increase. The greatest threat to cybersecurity in America, however, is complacency. There are some in the internet community who still believe that the internet can heal itself. This is just naïve. There are some business groups who argue that a disaggregated, voluntary approach to cybersecurity guided by information sharing will be adequate. This was tried in the Clinton administration. It did not work then, it does not work now, it will not work in the future when our opponents are more advanced and when we are more dependent on cyber space.

The future of threats in cyber space involves the diffusion and the commoditization of attack capabilities. It will involve an increased number of privacy breaches and the loss of intellectual property. There are a number of steps that could reduce these risks, but unfortunately it appears that we may need to wait for a damaging cyber attack to make us move.

I appreciate all the work the committee has done, both the full committee and the subcommittees. I know you are trying hard, but I think this attack is inevitable. Thank you for the opportunity to testify and I look forward to your questions.

[The prepared statement of Mr. Lewis follows:]

PREPARED STATEMENT OF JAMES A. LEWIS

APRIL 24, 2012

Every week—it's getting kind of boring—we read about hackers pilfering some company's database and stealing data on thousands or even millions of individuals. These are private-sector networks and they point to a crucial problem for assessing cybersecurity. Government agencies have to be transparent about breaches. Companies have to report breaches when it affects consumer privacy. But companies don't have to report breaches involving intellectual property or critical infrastructure. In fact, it is in their interest to conceal them. Perhaps the new Security and Exchange Commission Ruling that asks companies to report cyber incidents that damage shareholder value will change this, but it is too early to tell.

So we have frequent reports of penetrations to governments' systems, weekly or daily reports of penetrations of company networks that affect privacy, and almost no reports of penetrations affecting intellectual property and critical services. This pattern is not credible—the level of privacy-related penetrations companies report is likely to also be the real level of intellectual property-related penetration. It's just not reported. We know from anecdotal data and from a few published instances that these network penetrations occur frequently. This anomaly in the reporting suggests we really lack—in open-source information—a clear understanding of the threat to the American private sector, and that protestations that private networks are secure or do a better job are, to put it charitably, inaccurate.

An accurate assessment of threats in cyber space is essential for effective defense. A defense built on fictions will fail the first time it is tested. There is too much wishful thinking and complacency in the face of a threat that is growing as potential attackers acquire new capabilities and as our economy becomes more dependent on the internet and other cyber technologies. Digital networks are now the backbone of economic activity and National security, but our efforts to secure them remain haphazard, putting our Nation at risk. We can better understand this risk by looking at three separate categories of threat—espionage, crime, and attack.

Our adversaries include powerful states, skilful criminals, and a range of extremist groups. We are hampered in our defense against these opponents when we try to treat cybersecurity as a business problem. Some companies will take adequate defense measures; other will not. It makes business sense for an intelligence agency to spend lavishly to penetrate an opponent's network. It does not make business sense for companies to spend at the same rate to defend. To put this in military terms, we have an uncoordinated defense that is easy to defeat in detail.

Cyber espionage is the most pressing threat we face. The loss of intellectual property and business confidential information—economic espionage—using hacking and other techniques poses a threat to National security by undermining the military advantage provided by technology and by damaging economic competitiveness. The rate and degree to which National security is damaged depends, of course, on the ability of the acquiring nations to actually use the technology they steal and on America's own economic policies and Government support for science and engineering—our own economic policies and laws probably do more damage than cyber espionage—but there are many troubling incidents that suggest that real harm is being done. A major oil company lost exploration data worth hundreds of millions to a foreign attacker. We all know the Google case—at least 34 other high-tech companies were also penetrated, although they did not report the fact. Foreign hackers took IMF and G–20 documents relating to global financial negotiations. The delays and cost overruns in the F–35 program may be the result of cyber espionage, as could the rapid development of China's J–20 stealth fighter. Industries as diverse as chemicals, telecommunications, and solar energy have all suffered from cyber espionage.

The most harmful form of cyber espionage is state-directed. Foreign nation-state opponents are sophisticated intelligence agencies and advanced militaries whose business is to defeat network defenses and who have a demonstrated capacity to easily exploit commercial and Government networks. They have resources and persistence and their work can be seen as an extension of traditional espionage activities. Our network defenses are so poor, particularly in the "dot.com" space, that the effort to break in probably only takes these agencies and their proxies a few months of effort.

There is no convincing estimate of the cost of economic espionage to the United States. One study put the cost at perhaps $30 billion a year (in 2011 dollars) but other studies estimate the loss to be in the hundreds of billions. These higher figures exaggerate loss, but whatever the dollar figure, the illicit acquisition of technology and the loss of confidential political and business information hurts American security. The insight into Government policies, and strategic industries provided by cyber espionage, and the acceleration of competitor technological development, provide foreign competitors with a tangible advantage that harms the United States. The committee may wish to ask, for example, for classified briefing on improvements in China's stealth and submarine capabilities and the possible relation between these improvements and hacking incidents at defense contractors over the last decade.

We do not want to assume that losses are distributed evenly across all sectors of the economy. State-sponsored espionage will focus on area of concern to governments: Advanced technologies in aerospace, materials, information technology, and sensors, as well as commercially valuable financial data and energy-related information. Semiconductors and solar energy have been prime targets recently. Private entities also engage in cyber espionage, in many cases they do so with the acceptance of their governments. Hacking by private companies and individuals could engage a much broader swath of companies and technology. This probably reflects not only commercial interests but also an official policy to encourage the illicit acquisition of technology as a way to promote economic growth.

Cyber espionage ranks first as a threat to the United States and other developed countries. Cyber crimes focused on financial gain are a lesser threat, but they damage public safety by putting private citizens and companies at risk of monetary loss. Anecdotal evidence suggests that crime against banks and other financial institutions probably costs the United States a several hundred million dollars every year. This is not a major economic loss, but harms American citizens and does some damage to our economy. However, cyber crime also threatens National security in that it allows potential opponents to maintain and train proxy forces at our expense. Nations like Russia and China are sanctuaries for cyber crime because it allows them to maintain "irregular forces" in cyber space—hackers who can be tapped to do the state's bidding in espionage, coercion, or attack.

A recent opinion piece in a leading newspaper illustrates how confusing the discussion of cybersecurity has become, and helps explain why America may be too slow in constructing adequate defenses. The essay posited that most cyber criminals did not make much money, and that the threat they posed was overblown. You can test this formula by applying to it mugging: Most muggers do not make much money, so by the same logic, mugging is not a problem. This formula is divorced from any serious concept of public safety. Similarly, the National security implications of cyber crime were overlooked. Since cyber criminals are the proxy forces—the irregulars—that our two most dangerous opponents in cyber space use for National ends, cyber crime is an indirect and unwitting subsidies from American companies to foreign military and intelligence services.

Cyber espionage and crime happen on a daily basis. This is [sic] nto the for [sic] cyber attacks against critical infrastructure or services, which have been few and far between. The threat comes from the spread of attack capabilities. In 2007, tests at the Idaho National Labs showed that sending malicious instructions via computer networks to the industrial control systems used to run critical infrastructure could cause machines to destroy themselves. Stuxnet produced a similar effect. These incidents showed that software can be sued as a weapon, and the internet as a delivery vehicle. Espionage and crime exploit vulnerabilities in networks technologies; attacks on critical infrastructure compound this by exploiting not only network vulnerabilities but also the vulnerabilities in industrial control systems. There is no economic incentive to fix these control vulnerabilities because they will not affect normal operations and they will become visible only when there is an attack. While the cost of cyber crime is relatively small, it is an integral part of other, more dangerous threat we face, including the ability to launch a damaging cyber attack.

These attacks have been long prophesied, but we have only seen two or three. Only a few nations have the capability to destroy critical infrastructure and they are unlikely to use it outside of a war. We know that our two most likely military opponents have the capability to penetrate networks, scramble data, disrupt critical services, and even cause physical damage. We also know that they are more deterrable, more responsible, and in the case of China, face major disincentives, as a disruptive cyber attack would do as much damage to their own country, given how deeply our two nations' economies are intertwined.

You sometimes hear analysts say that we are in a covert cyber war with China. This is inaccurate. We should stop trying to cram our complicated relationship with China into a simple Cold War framework. China and the United States are interdependent in ways that were inconceivable for the United States and Soviet Union. China is challenging the United States, but it is not a peer-competitor. Although it is rapidly increasing its military capabilities, it does not pose the existential threat to the United States that the Soviet Union posed. Given the deep distrust and hostility between the two nations, and the competition for regional and global influence, cybersecurity is a potential flashpoint in the bilateral relationship and a source of growing tension, but this is not war.

The number of nations seeking to acquire cyber attack capabilities is growing rapidly—cyber attack is becoming a standard element in military planning. A more troubling development is that new classes of opponents are seeking the ability to launch cyber attacks. These new classes of opponents will not be as easily constrained. They are more likely to use cyber attack and all evidence suggests that we have nothing in the way of adequate defense. We simply do not take the threat of cyber attack seriously—would anyone not paid to do so argue that information sharing and voluntary action would protect us from terrorism? Or that telling companies what missiles and aircraft look like would be an adequate defense against a nuclear strike? But it is an American tradition to be surprised by opponents and only take action after the first attack.

The area of greatest concern is in the diffusion of the ability to attack critical infrastructure, to less responsible and less deterrable actors who may calculate that it is in their interest to launch a cyber attack against the United States. Attack capabilities could spread if private hackers to independently discover the techniques currently possessed by governments. Some members of the hacker community have amazing capabilities. Another way attack capabilities could spread would be for hackers who are government proxies in Russia and China to "commercialize" the skills and tools they have been provided for official purposes. These proxies receive training and support from military and intelligence agencies. They also participate in the cyber crime black markets. The flow from government agencies to proxies to the black market is likely, although it appears that governments still reserve the most advanced attack technique to themselves.

It is difficult to assess how rapidly attack capabilities are growing outside of governments, and the actual transmission mechanism for cyber attack tools is unclear. For example, more than a decade ago, foreign intelligence agencies had the ability to activate cell phones and use them as listening devices even if they were turned off. Variants of this technique appear to be entering the black market. We do not know if it is because someone is commercializing a skill they learned from government service or if it is an independent discovery. People play with the technology and code—this is the original meaning of hacking—and find how to do interesting things the designers never intended or suspected were possible.

The most advanced exploits are still out of reach, however, for all but large, well-resourced attackers. Stuxnet, for example, combined deep engineering knowledge and clandestine intelligence techniques with advanced hacking skills. Private hackers and most governments do not yet have the capability to launch a Stuxnet-like attack (but this is coming). That some of the Stuxnet code is publicly available does not really increase risk. Many cyber attacks are "single-use" exploits that work as a surprise but are much less effective after the target reacts and adjusts. In the United States, for example, a 2010 survey found that three-quarters of American utilities said they had put in place defenses against Stuxnet. These utilities would most likely be able to deflect a Stuxnet-like attack, while only the others would still be vulnerable.

Stuxnet has increased risk as it has shown the world how to stage a damaging cyber attack, but there are many options other than Stuxnet. Unfortunately, even private hackers can exploit freely available information on vulnerabilities and penetration techniques to attack many commercial networks and the critical infrastructure connected to them. Why use an advanced attack like Stuxnet when a simple attack will work so well? There are tools that allow anyone to scan the internet to find unprotected digital devices at critical infrastructure facilities that connect control systems to the internet. You can scan for devices that are improperly configured, devices such as wireless routers that come from the manufacturer with the password set as "password." It does not take a mastermind to break into such systems.

These tools are widely available. Informal tests using these tools can find several thousand insecure connections in the United States on any given day. They provide a "consumer version" of the cyber reconnaissance an advanced power would carry out in planning an attack against the United States. Combine these publicly available reconnaissance tools with attack tools available on the cyber crime black market, and anyone with sufficiently advanced hacking skills will be able to attack poorly defended critical infrastructure or other commercial targets.

The diffusion and consumerization of attack capabilities is not the only growing source of threat. We must also consider motivation and intent, in addition to capability. The few nations that currently possess advanced cyber attack capabilities are deterred by American military force or they are our allies. Most cyber criminals only engage in actions that generate income. Attacking critical infrastructure does not generate income unless extortion is involved (by threatening to disrupt services if the criminal is not paid). Cyber criminals have no motive to launch a cyber attack unless they are acting as government proxies or unless they have been hired as mercenaries.

This is where the nexus between the diffusion of attack capabilities and intent become important. There are countries and groups that would like to attack the United States and are not as deterrable as our current adversaries. As nations and hackers develop more sophisticated attack capabilities and as sophisticated attack tools become available on the cyber crime black market, the threat of attack is increasing.

We know that two countries hostile to the United States are developing cyber attack capabilities. North Korea has been pursuing cyber capabilities for more than a decade but the backwardness of its economy has so far limited its success. North Korea lacks easy access to advanced technologies. Its tightly controlled population is an unlikely source of hackers, as North Koreans do not have the independence and internet access hackers need to thrive. Technological backwardness and political culture are major obstacles to developing strong hacking capabilities, but, as with nuclear weapons, if North Korea is able to support sustained investment in cyber attack capabilities and find some outside support, it will eventually acquire them. North Korea's erratic behavior suggests it will use cyber attacks against South Korea, Japan, or U.S. forces in Korea, should it succeed in its long quest to obtain a cyber attack capability.

Iran is a more troubling case. Iran has also been pursing the acquisition of cyber attack capabilities for several years. Iran has been for many years willing to attack U.S. forces and embassies in the region, and FBI Director Mueller stated in recent testimony that Iran is more willing to carry out attacks inside the United States. Statements by Iranian officials show that they believe that the United States, along with Israel, was responsible for the Stuxnet attacks and suggest that they believe they would be justified in retaliating in kind. Iran's attack capabilities are still limited but they have probed Israeli networks in what appear to be tests. Iranian hackers have greater access to the internet and to the cyber black market than North Korea, suggesting that their development of cyber capabilities will be more rapid.

Iran, even more than North Korea, could miscalculate the costs of a cyber attack against the United States. Iran has groups that it sponsors, like Hezbollah, that it has used in the past to attack Americans. The Iranians may believe that these proxies will make it difficult for the United States to attribute an attack and this will reduce their perceptions of the risk of a cyber attack on American targets. Iran routinely exaggerates its military capabilities and its claims of cyber prowess are dubious, but there is a clear commitment (as with nuclear weapons) by the regime to continue its efforts to acquire the ability to launch cyber attacks.

Finally there are non-state, anti-American and activist groups that already make extensive use of the internet. As cyber attack capabilities become "commoditized," the temptation for these politically motivated groups to use them against vulnerable U.S. targets will increase. We have not seen terrorist groups use cyber attacks—they seem to have neither the capability nor the interest—but since these groups make extensive use of the internet they could eventually be attracted to cyber attack if the means to carry it out are easily available. Some non-state actors are grouped under the label "Anonymous," a disparate and decentralized federation of internet activists where many members espouse anti-government or anti-American ideas. The name "Anonymous" is misleading, however, as it implies a single entity. Anyone can say they are "Anonymous," from individuals posting comments on 4Chan to members of foreign intelligence agencies (for whom "false flag" operations are routine). In a few cases, it appears that cyber criminals have used the name Anonymous when carrying out their for-profit exploits.

These threats are all external, but greatest threat to America's cybersecurity come from inside. This threat is complacency and it has two sources. In the internet community, there are many who still believe that the internet can heal itself, that civil society and multi-stakeholder internet governance will ultimately provide adequate security. They say that threats in cyber space are exaggerated and that better cybersecurity puts privacy and the alleged virtues of an open internet for innovation at risk. This is simply naïve and outdated. This sort of approach has never worked anywhere else, and it is not working now in cyber space.

At the same time, business groups underestimate the threat we face and continue to assert that some sort of disaggregated, voluntary approach to cybersecurity, guided by better information sharing, will be adequate to protect the Nation. This, of course, was the approach adopted by the Clinton administration in 1998. It did not work then and it does not work now. It will not work in the future when our opponents are even more advanced and when we are even more dependent on cyber space. Simplifying the regulatory and tax structure would be immensely beneficial for our economy, but it is a non-sequitur to argue that blocking mandatory standards for cybersecurity somehow compensates for any over-regulation of commercial activities.

The future of threats in cyber space will involve the diffusion and commoditization of attack capabilities. It will involve an increased number of privacy breaches and the loss of intellectual property and confidential business information. The situation is not static and could change rapidly. There are a number of steps we could take to reduce risk, but these steps face insurmountable political obstacles that will not disappear until after a damaging cyber event. To prepare itself for the inevitable, the committee may wish to ask for a classified briefing on the best available intelligence estimate for when America will experience a cyber attack.

Mr. McCAUL. Thank you, Jim, for your testimony and your service to the country on this important issue.

With that, the Chairman now recognizes Mr. Wilshusen.

STATEMENT OF GREGORY C. WILSHUSEN, DIRECTOR, INFORMATION SECURITY ISSUES, GOVERNMENT ACCOUNTABILITY OFFICE

Mr. WILSHUSEN. Chairman McCaul, Ranking Member Keating, and Members of the subcommittee, thank you for the opportunity to testify at today's hearing on cyber-based threats facing our Nation. The increasing dependency of IT systems and network operations pervades nearly every aspect of our society. In particular, increasing network interconnectivity has revolutionized the way our Government, our Nation, and much of the world communicate and conduct business. While bringing significant benefits, this dependency also creates vulnerabilities to cyber-based threats. Today I will describe some of those threats, vulnerabilities, and reported security incidents affecting the Nation's systems.

But first, if I may, Mr. Chairman, I would like to recognize several members of my team who were instrumental in preparing this statement. One, Mike Gilmore, is behind me. Back at the office Anjalique Lawrence, Lee McCracken, and Kristi Dorsey played a pivotal role in developing these statements.

Mr. Chairman, the Nation faces an evolving array of cyber-based threats. These threats can be intentional and/or unintentional. Unintentional threats can be caused by software upgrades or defective equipment that inadvertently disrupt systems. Intentional threats can involve targeted and untargeted attacks from a variety of sources. These sources, as have been mentioned earlier, include foreign nations, criminal groups, hackers, terrorists, and insiders. They vary in their capabilities and their motives, which include seeking monetary gain and pursuing an economic, political, or military advantage. Moreover they have a variety of attack techniques at their disposal, such as using malicious code, social engineering, phishing, denial of service, and more sophisticated attacks that can use a combination of these and other techniques. The nature of these attacks vastly enhances the reach and impact due to the fact that attackers do not need to be physically close to victims and can more easily remain anonymous.

The threat posed by cyber attacks is heightened by vulnerabilities in Federal systems and networks. Specifically, significant weaknesses in security controls continue to threaten the confidentiality, integrity, and availability of information systems supporting Federal operations.

Most major Federal agencies have significant deficiencies in their information security controls. For fiscal year 2011, 18 of the 24 major Federal agencies reported inadequate information system controls for financial reporting purposes, and inspectors general at 22 of these agencies identified information security as a major management challenge for their agency. GAO and agency IGs have made hundreds of recommendations to agencies to strengthen controls over their systems.

We have also identified vulnerabilities and industrial control systems that monitor and control sensitive processes and physical functions supporting the Nation's critical infrastructures. Federal agencies continue to report an increasing number of cybersecurity incidents. Over the past 6 years, the number of incidents reported by Federal agencies to US–CERT has risen nearly 680 percent, to almost 42,900 in fiscal year 2011. These incidents include unauthorized access and improper use of computing resources and the installation of malicious software on systems. Reported attacks and unintentional incidents involving Federal, private, and critical infrastructure systems occur daily and demonstrate that their impact can be serious.

For example, individuals could suffer privacy and financial loss from identity theft and on-line scams. Private companies could lose a competitive advantage or market value from the cyber threat of intellectual property or business proprietary information, and essential Government functions and critical infrastructure services could be impaired or disrupted.

In summary, the cyber threats facing the Nation are evolving and growing with a wide array of threat actors having access to increasingly sophisticated techniques for exploiting system vulnerabilities. The danger posed by these threats is heightened by the weaknesses that pervade Federal information systems and systems supporting critical infrastructures. Ensuring the security of these systems is essential to limiting potentially devastating consequences that imperil public health and safety in our National and economic security.

Mr. Chairman, this completes my statement. I would be happy to answer any questions.

[The prepared statement of Mr. Wilshusen follows:]

PREPARED STATEMENT OF GREGORY C. WILSHUSEN

APRIL 24, 2012

GAO HIGHLIGHTS

Highlights of GAO–12–666T, a testimony before the Subcommittee on Oversight, Investigations, and Management, Committee on Homeland Security, House of Representatives.

Why GAO Did This Study

Nearly every aspect of American society increasingly depends upon information technology systems and networks. This includes increasing computer interconnectivity, particularly through the widespread use of the internet as a medium of communication and commerce. While providing significant benefits, this increased interconnectivity can also create vulnerabilities to cyber-based threats. Pervasive and sustained cyber attacks against the United States could have a potentially devastating impact on Federal and non-Federal systems, disrupting the operations of governments and businesses and the lives of private individuals. Accordingly, GAO has designated Federal information security as a Government-wide high-risk area since 1997, and in 2003 expanded it to include protecting systems and assets vital to the Nation (referred to as critical infrastructures).

GAO is providing a statement that describes: (1) Cyber threats facing the Nation's systems, (2) vulnerabilities present in Federal information systems and systems supporting critical infrastructure, and (3) reported cyber incidents and their impacts. In preparing this statement, GAO relied on previously published work in these areas and reviewed more recent GAO, agency, and inspectors general work, as well as reports on security incidents.

What GAO Recommends

GAO has previously made recommendations to resolve identified significant control deficiencies.

CYBERSECURITY.—THREATS IMPACTING THE NATION

What GAO Found

The Nation faces an evolving array of cyber-based threats arising from a variety of sources. These threats can be intentional or unintentional. Unintentional threats can be caused by software upgrades or defective equipment that inadvertently disrupt systems, and intentional threats can be both targeted and untargeted attacks from a variety of threat sources. Sources of threats include criminal groups, hackers, terrorists, organization insiders, and foreign nations engaged in crime, political activism, or espionage and information warfare. These threat sources vary in terms of the capabilities of the actors, their willingness to act, and their motives, which can include monetary gain or political advantage, among others. Moreover, potential threat actors have a variety of attack techniques at their disposal, which can adversely affect computers, software, a network, an organization's operation, an industry, or the internet itself. The nature of cyber attacks can vastly enhance their reach and impact due to the fact that attackers do not need to be physically close to their victims and can more easily remain anonymous, among other things. The magnitude of the threat is compounded by the ever-increasing sophistication of cyber attack techniques, such as attacks that may combine multiple techniques. Using these techniques, threat actors may target individuals, businesses, critical infrastructures, or Government organizations.

The threat posed by cyber attacks is heightened by vulnerabilities in Federal systems and systems supporting critical infrastructure. Specifically, significant weaknesses in information security controls continue to threaten the confidentiality, integrity, and availability of critical information and information systems supporting the operations, assets, and personnel of Federal Government agencies. For example, 18 of 24 major Federal agencies have reported inadequate information security controls for financial reporting for fiscal year 2011, and inspectors general at 22 of these agencies identified information security as a major management challenge for their agency. Moreover, GAO, agency, and inspector general assessments of information security controls during fiscal year 2011 revealed that most major agencies had weaknesses in most major categories of information system controls. In addition, GAO has identified vulnerabilities in systems that monitor and control sensitive processes and physical functions supporting the Nation's critical infrastructures. These and similar weaknesses can be exploited by threat actors, with potentially severe effects.

The number of cybersecurity incidents reported by Federal agencies continues to rise, and recent incidents illustrate that these pose serious risk. Over the past 6 years, the number of incidents reported by Federal agencies to the Federal information security incident center has increased by nearly 680 percent. These incidents include unauthorized access to systems; improper use of computing resources; and the installation of malicious software, among others. Reported attacks and unintentional incidents involving Federal, private, and infrastructure systems demonstrate that the impact of a serious attack could be significant, including loss of personal or sensitive information, disruption or destruction of critical infrastructure, and damage to National and economic security.

Chairman McCaul, Ranking Member Keating, and Members of the subcommittee: Thank you for the opportunity to testify at today's hearing on the cyber-based threats facing our Nation.

The increasing dependency upon information technology (IT) systems and networked operations pervades nearly every aspect of our society. In particular, increasing computer interconnectivity—most notably growth in the use of the internet—has revolutionized the way that our Government, our Nation, and much of the world communicate and conduct business. While bringing significant benefits, this dependency can also create vulnerabilities to cyber-based threats. Pervasive and sustained cyber attacks against the United States could have a potentially devastating impact on Federal and non-Federal systems and operations. In January 2012, the Director of National Intelligence testified that such threats pose a critical National and economic security concern.[1] These growing and evolving threats can potentially affect all segments of our society—individuals; private businesses; local, State, and Federal governments; and other entities. Underscoring the importance of this issue, we have designated Federal information security as a high-risk area since 1997 and in 2003 expanded this area to include protecting computerized systems supporting our Nation's critical infrastructure.[2]

In my testimony today, I will describe: (1) Cyber threats facing the Nation's systems, (2) vulnerabilities present in Federal systems and systems supporting critical infrastructure,[3] and (3) reported cyber incidents and their impacts. In preparing this statement in April 2012, we relied on our previous work in these areas. (Please see the related GAO products in appendix I.) These products contain detailed overviews of the scope and methodology we used. We also reviewed more recent agency, inspector general, and GAO assessments of security vulnerabilities at Federal agencies and information on security incidents from the U.S. Computer Emergency Readiness Team (US–CERT), media reports, and other publicly available sources. The work on which this statement is based was conducted in accordance with generally accepted Government auditing standards. Those standards require that we plan and perform audits to obtain sufficient, appropriate evidence to provide a reasonable basis for our findings and conclusions based on our audit objectives. We believe that the evidence obtained provided a reasonable basis for our findings and conclusions based on our audit objectives.

BACKGROUND

As computer technology has advanced, both Government and private entities have become increasingly dependent on computerized information systems to carry out operations and to process, maintain, and report essential information. Public and

---

[1] James R. Clapper, Director of National Intelligence, Unclassified Statement for the Record on the Worldwide Threat Assessment of the U.S. Intelligence Community for the Senate Select Committee on Intelligence (January 31, 2012).

[2] See, most recently, GAO, *High-Risk Series: An Update,* GAO–11–278 (Washington, DC: February, 2011).

[3] Critical infrastructures are systems and assets, whether physical or virtual, so vital to our Nation that their incapacity or destruction would have a debilitating impact on National security, economic well-being, public health or safety, or any combination of these.

private organizations rely on computer systems to transmit sensitive and proprietary information, develop and maintain intellectual capital, conduct operations, process business transactions, transfer funds, and deliver services. In addition, the internet has grown increasingly important to American business and consumers, serving as a medium for hundreds of billions of dollars of commerce each year, as well as developing into an extended information and communications infrastructure supporting vital services such as power distribution, health care, law enforcement, and National defense.

Consequently, the security of these systems and networks is essential to protecting National and economic security, public health and safety, and the flow of commerce. Conversely, ineffective information security controls can result in significant risks, including:

- loss or theft of resources, such as Federal payments and collections;
- inappropriate access to and disclosure, modification, or destruction of sensitive information, such as National security information, personal taxpayer information, or proprietary business information;
- disruption of critical operations supporting critical infrastructure, National defense, or emergency services;
- undermining of agency missions due to embarrassing incidents that erode the public's confidence in Government; and
- use of computer resources for unauthorized purposes or to launch attacks on other computers' systems.

THE NATION FACES AN EVOLVING ARRAY OF CYBER-BASED THREATS

Cyber-based threats are evolving and growing and arise from a wide array of sources. These threats can be unintentional or intentional. Unintentional threats can be caused by software upgrades or defective equipment that inadvertently disrupt systems. Intentional threats include both targeted and untargeted attacks from a variety of sources, including criminal groups, hackers, disgruntled employees, foreign nations engaged in espionage and information warfare, and terrorists. These threat sources vary in terms of the capabilities of the actors, their willingness to act, and their motives, which can include monetary gain or political advantage, among others. Table 1 shows common sources of cyber threats.

TABLE 1.—SOURCES OF CYBERSECURITY THREATS

Threat Source	Description
Bot-network operators	Bot-net operators use a network, or bot-net, of compromised, remotely-controlled systems to coordinate attacks and to distribute phishing schemes, spam, and malware attacks. The services of these networks are sometimes made available on underground markets (e.g., purchasing a denial-of-service attack or services to relay spam or phishing attacks).
Criminal groups	Criminal groups seek to attack systems for monetary gain. Specifically, organized criminal groups use spam, phishing, and spyware/malware to commit identity theft, on-line fraud, and computer extortion. International corporate spies and criminal organizations also pose a threat to the United States through their ability to conduct industrial espionage and large-scale monetary theft and to hire or develop hacker talent.

TABLE 1.—SOURCES OF CYBERSECURITY THREATS—Continued

Threat Source	Description
Hackers	Hackers break into networks for the thrill of the challenge, bragging rights in the hacker community, revenge, stalking, monetary gain, and political activism, among other reasons. While gaining unauthorized access once required a fair amount of skill or computer knowledge, hackers can now download attack scripts and protocols from the internet and launch them against victim sites. Thus, while attack tools have become more sophisticated, they have also become easier to use. According to the Central Intelligence Agency, the large majority of hackers do not have the requisite expertise to threaten difficult targets such as critical U.S. networks. Nevertheless, the world-wide population of hackers poses a relatively high threat of an isolated or brief disruption causing serious damage.
Insiders	The disgruntled organization insider is a principal source of computer crime. Insiders may not need a great deal of knowledge about computer intrusions because their knowledge of a target system often allows them to gain unrestricted access to cause damage to the system or to steal system data. The insider threat includes contractors hired by the organization, as well as careless or poorly-trained employees who may inadvertently introduce malware into systems.
Nations	Nations use cyber tools as part of their information-gathering and espionage activities. In addition, several nations are aggressively working to develop information warfare doctrine, programs, and capabilities. Such capabilities enable a single entity to have a significant and serious impact by disrupting the supply, communications, and economic infrastructures that support military power—impacts that could affect the daily lives of citizens across the country. In his January 2012 testimony, the Director of National Intelligence stated that, among state actors, China and Russia are of particular concern.
Phishers	Individuals or small groups execute phishing schemes in an attempt to steal identities or information for monetary gain. Phishers may also use spam and spyware or malware to accomplish their objectives.
Spammers	Individuals or organizations distribute unsolicited e-mail with hidden or false information in order to sell products, conduct phishing schemes, distribute spyware or malware, or attack organizations (e.g., a denial of service).
Spyware or malware authors.	Individuals or organizations with malicious intent carry out attacks against users by producing and distributing spyware and malware. Several destructive computer viruses and worms have harmed files and hard drives, including the Melissa Macro Virus, the Explore.Zip worm, the CIH (Chernobyl) Virus, Nimda, Code Red, Slammer, and Blaster.
Terrorists	Terrorists seek to destroy, incapacitate, or exploit critical infrastructures in order to threaten National security, cause mass casualties, weaken the economy, and damage public morale and confidence. Terrorists may use phishing schemes or spyware/malware in order to generate funds or gather sensitive information.

Source: GAO analysis based on data from the Director of National Intelligence, Department of Justice, Central Intelligence Agency, and the Software Engineering Institute's CERT® Coordination Center.

These sources of cyber threats make use of various techniques, or exploits, that may adversely affect computers, software, a network, an organization's operation, an industry, or the internet itself. Table 2 provides descriptions of common types of cyber exploits.

TABLE 2.—TYPES OF CYBER EXPLOITS

Type of Exploit	Description
Cross-site scripting	An attack that uses third-party web resources to run script within the victim's web browser or scriptable application. This occurs when a browser visits a malicious website or clicks a malicious link. The most dangerous consequences occur when this method is used to exploit additional vulnerabilities that may permit an attacker to steal cookies (data exchanged between a web server and a browser), log key strokes, capture screen shots, discover and collect network information, and remotely access and control the victim's machine.
Denial-of-service	An attack that prevents or impairs the authorized use of networks, systems, or applications by exhausting resources.
Distributed denial-of-service.	A variant of the denial-of-service attack that uses numerous hosts to perform the attack.
Logic bombs	A piece of programming code intentionally inserted into a software system that will cause a malicious function to occur when one or more specified conditions are met.
Phishing	A digital form of social engineering that uses authentic-looking, but fake, e-mails to request information from users or direct them to a fake website that requests information.
Passive wiretapping ...	The monitoring or recording of data, such as passwords transmitted in clear text, while they are being transmitted over a communications link. This is done without altering or affecting the data.
Structured Query Language (SQL) injection.	An attack that involves the alteration of a database search in a web-based application, which can be used to obtain unauthorized access to sensitive information in a database.
Trojan horse	A computer program that appears to have a useful function, but also has a hidden and potentially malicious function that evades security mechanisms by, for example, masquerading as a useful program that a user would likely execute.
Virus	A computer program that can copy itself and infect a computer without the permission or knowledge of the user. A virus might corrupt or delete data on a computer, use e-mail programs to spread itself to other computers, or even erase everything on a hard disk. Unlike a computer worm, a virus requires human involvement (usually unwitting) to propagate.
War driving	The method of driving through cities and neighborhoods with a wireless-equipped computer—sometimes with a powerful antenna—searching for unsecured wireless networks.
Worm	A self-replicating, self-propagating, self-contained program that uses network mechanisms to spread itself. Unlike computer viruses, worms do not require human involvement to propagate.
Zero-day exploit	An exploit that takes advantage of a security vulnerability previously unknown to the general public. In many cases, the exploit code is written by the same person who discovered the vulnerability. By writing an exploit for the previously unknown vulnerability, the attacker creates a potent threat since the compressed time frame between public discoveries of both makes it difficult to defend against.

Source: GAO analysis of data from the National Institute of Standards and Technology, United States Computer Emergency Readiness Team, and industry reports.

The unique nature of cyber-based attacks can vastly enhance their reach and impact. For example, cyber attackers do not need to be physically close to their victims, technology allows attacks to easily cross State and National borders, attacks can be carried out at high speed and directed at a number of victims simultaneously, and cyber attackers can more easily remain anonymous. Moreover, the use of these and other techniques is becoming more sophisticated, with attackers using multiple or "blended" approaches that combine two or more techniques. Using these techniques, threat actors may target individuals, resulting in loss of privacy or identity theft; businesses, resulting in the compromise of proprietary information or intellectual capital; critical infrastructures, resulting in their disruption or destruction; or Government agencies, resulting in the loss of sensitive information and damage to economic and National security.

SYSTEMS SUPPORTING FEDERAL OPERATIONS AND CRITICAL INFRASTRUCTURE ARE VULNERABLE TO CYBER ATTACKS

Significant weaknesses in information security controls continue to threaten the confidentiality, integrity, and availability of critical information and information systems used to support the operations, assets, and personnel of Federal agencies. For example, in their performance and accountability reports and annual financial reports for fiscal year 2011, 18 of 24 major Federal agencies[4] indicated that inadequate information security controls were either material weaknesses or significant deficiencies[5] for financial reporting purposes. In addition, inspectors general at 22 of the major agencies identified information security or information system control as a major management challenge for their agency.

Agency, inspectors general, and GAO assessments of information security controls during fiscal year 2011 revealed that most major Federal agencies had weaknesses in most of the five major categories of information system controls: (1) Access controls, which ensure that only authorized individuals can read, alter, or delete data; (2) configuration management controls, which provide assurance that only authorized software programs are implemented; (3) segregation of duties, which reduces the risk that one individual can independently perform inappropriate actions without detection; (4) continuity of operations planning, which helps avoid significant disruptions in computer-dependent operations; and (5) agency-wide information security programs, which provide a framework for ensuring that risks are understood and that effective controls are selected and implemented. Figure 1 shows the number of agencies that had vulnerabilities in these five information security control categories.

---

[4] The 24 major departments and agencies are the Departments of Agriculture, Commerce, Defense, Education, Energy, Health and Human Services, Homeland Security, Housing and Urban Development, the Interior, Justice, Labor, State, Transportation, the Treasury, and Veterans Affairs; the Environmental Protection Agency, General Services Administration, National Aeronautics and Space Administration, National Science Foundation, Nuclear Regulatory Commission, Office of Personnel Management, Small Business Administration, Social Security Administration, and U.S. Agency for International Development.

[5] A material weakness is a deficiency, or a combination of deficiencies, in internal control such that there is a reasonable possibility that a material misstatement of the entity's financial statements will not be prevented, or detected and corrected on a timely basis. A significant deficiency is a deficiency, or a combination of deficiencies, in internal control that is less severe than a material weakness, yet important enough to merit attention by those charged with governance. A control deficiency exists when the design or operation of a control does not allow management or employees, in the normal course of performing their assigned functions, to prevent, or detect and correct, misstatements on a timely basis.

Figure 1: Information Security Weaknesses at 24 Major Federal Agencies in Fiscal Year 2011

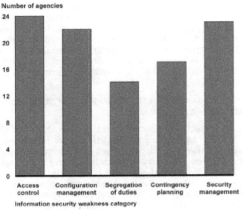

Source: GAO analysis of agency, inspectors general, and GAO reports.

Over the past several years, we and agency inspectors general have made hundreds of recommendations to resolve similar previously identified significant control deficiencies. We have also recommended that agencies fully implement comprehensive, agency-wide information security programs, including by correcting weaknesses in specific areas of their programs. The effective implementation of these recommendations will strengthen the security posture at these agencies.

In addition, securing the control systems that monitor and control sensitive processes and physical functions supporting many of our Nation's critical infrastructures is a National priority, and we have identified vulnerabilities in these systems. For example, in September 2007, we reported that critical infrastructure control systems faced increasing risks due to cyber threats, system vulnerabilities, and the serious potential impact of possible attacks.[6] Specifically, we determined that critical infrastructure owners faced both technical and organizational challenges to securing control systems, such as limited processing capabilities and developing compelling business cases for investing in control systems security, among others. We further identified Federal initiatives under way to help secure these control systems, but noted that more needed to be done to coordinate these efforts and address shortfalls. We made recommendations to the Department of Homeland Security to develop a strategy for coordinating control systems security efforts and enhance information sharing with relevant stakeholders. Since this report, the Department formed the Industrial Control Systems Cyber Emergency Response Team to provide industrial control system stakeholders with situational awareness and analytical support to effectively manage risk. In addition, it has taken several actions, such as developing a catalog of recommended security practices for control systems, developing a cybersecurity evaluation tool that allows asset owners to assess their control systems and overall security posture, and collaborating with others to promote control standards and system security. We have not evaluated these activities to assess their effectiveness in improving the security of control systems against cyber threats.

In May 2008, we reported that the Tennessee Valley Authority's (TVA) corporate network contained security weaknesses that could lead to the disruption of control systems networks and devices connected to that network.[7] We made 19 recommendations to improve the implementation of information security program activities for the control systems governing TVA's critical infrastructures and 73 recommendations to address weaknesses in information security controls. TVA concurred with the recommendations and has taken steps to implement them.

In addition to those present in Federal systems and systems supporting critical infrastructure, vulnerabilities in mobile computing devices used by individuals or or-

---

[6] GAO, *Critical Infrastructure Protection: Multiple Efforts to Secure Control Systems Are Under Way, but Challenges Remain*, GAO–07–1036 (Washington, DC: Sept. 10, 2007).

[7] GAO, *Information Security: TVA Needs to Address Weaknesses in Control Systems and Networks*, GAO–08–526 (Washington, DC: May 21, 2008).

ganizations may provide openings to cyber threats. For example, consumers and Federal agencies are increasing their use of mobile devices to communicate and access services over the internet. The use of these devices offers many benefits including ease of sending and checking messages and remotely accessing information online; however, it can also introduce information security risks if not properly protected. We have on-going work to determine: (1) What common security threats and vulnerabilities affect generally available cellphones, smartphones, and tablets; (2) what security features and practices have been identified to mitigate the risks associated with these vulnerabilities; and (3) the extent to which Government and private entities are addressing security vulnerabilities of mobile devices.

NUMBER OF CYBERSECURITY INCIDENTS REPORTED BY FEDERAL AGENCIES CONTINUES TO RISE, AND RECENT INCIDENTS ILLUSTRATE SERIOUS RISK

Federal agencies have reported increasing numbers of security incidents that placed sensitive information at risk, with potentially serious impacts on Federal operations, assets, and people. When incidents occur, agencies are to notify the Federal information security incident center—US–CERT. Over the past 6 years, the number of incidents reported by Federal agencies to US–CERT has increased from 5,503 incidents in fiscal year 2006 to 42,887 incidents in fiscal year 2011, an increase of nearly 680 percent (see fig. 2).[8]

Figure 2: Incidents Reported to US-CERT: Fiscal Years 2006-2011

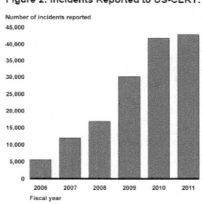

Source: GAO analysis of US-CERT data for fiscal years 2006-2011

Agencies reported the types of incidents and events based on US–CERT-defined categories. As indicated in figure 3, the two most prevalent types of incidents and events reported to US–CERT during fiscal year 2011 were unconfirmed incidents under investigation and malicious code.

---

[8] According to US–CERT, the growth in the number of incidents is attributable, in part, to agencies improving detection and reporting of security incidents on their respective networks.

Figure 3: Types of Incidents Reported to US-CERT in Fiscal Year 2011 by Category

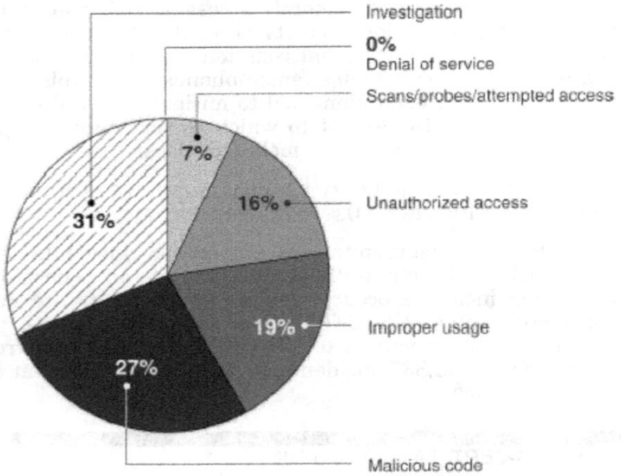

- Investigation
- **0%** Denial of service
- Scans/probes/attempted access — 7%
- Unauthorized access — 16%
- Improper usage — 19%
- Malicious code — 27%
- 31%

GAO analysis of US-CERT data for fiscal year 2011.

Reported attacks and unintentional incidents involving Federal, private, and critical infrastructure systems demonstrate that the impact of a serious attack could be significant. These agencies and organizations have experienced a wide range of incidents involving data loss or theft, computer intrusions, and privacy breaches, underscoring the need for improved security practices. The following examples from news media and other public sources illustrate that a broad array of information and assets remain at risk.

- In April 2012, hackers breached a server at the Utah Department of Health to access thousands of Medicaid records. Included in the breach were Medicaid recipients and clients of the Children's Health Insurance Plan. About 280,000 people had their Social Security numbers exposed. In addition, another 350,000 people listed in the eligibility inquiries may have had other sensitive data stolen, including names, birth dates, and addresses.
- In March 2012, it was reported that a security breach at Global Payments, a firm that processed payments for Visa and Mastercard, could compromise the credit- and debit-card information of millions of Americans. Subsequent to the reported breach, the company's stock fell more than 9 percent before trading in its stock was halted. Visa also removed the company from its list of approved processors.
- In February 2012, the inspector general at the National Aeronautics and Space Administration testified that an unencrypted notebook computer had been stolen from the agency in March 2011. The theft resulted in the loss of the algorithms used to command and control the International Space Station.
- In March 2012, a news wire service reported that the senior commander of the North Atlantic Treaty Organization (NATO) had been the target of repeated cyber attacks using the social networking website Facebook that were believed to have originated in China. According to the article, hackers repeatedly tried to dupe those close to the commander by setting up fake Facebook accounts in his name in the hope that his acquaintances would make contact and answer private messages, potentially divulging sensitive information about the commander or themselves.
- In March 2012, it was reported that Blue Cross Blue Shield of Tennessee paid out a settlement of $1.5 million to the U.S. Department of Health and Human Services arising from potential violations stemming from the theft of 57 unencrypted computer hard drives that contained protected health information of over 1 million individuals.
- In January 2012, the Department of Commerce discovered that the computer network of the Department's Economic Development Administration (EDA) was hit with a virus, forcing EDA to disable e-mail services and internet access pending investigation into the cause and scope of the problem, which persisted for over 12 weeks.

- In June 2011, a major bank reported that hackers had broken into its systems and gained access to the personal information of hundreds of thousands of customers. Through the bank's on-line banking system, the attackers were able to view certain private customer information.
- Citi reissued over 200,000 cards after a May 2011 website breach. About 360,000 of its approximately 23.5 million North American card accounts were affected, resulting in the potential for misuse of cardholder personal information.
- In April 2011, Sony disclosed that it suffered a massive breach in its video game on-line network that led to the theft of personal information, including the names, addresses, and possibly credit card data belonging to 77 million user accounts.
- In February 2011, media reports stated that computer hackers had broken into and stolen proprietary information worth millions of dollars from the networks of six U.S. and European energy companies.
- In July 2010, a sophisticated computer attack, known as Stuxnet, was discovered. It targeted control systems used to operate industrial processes in the energy, nuclear, and other critical sectors, reportedly causing physical damage. It is designed to exploit a combination of vulnerabilities to gain access to its target and modify code to change the process.
- A retailer reported in May 2011 that it had suffered a breach of its customers' card data. The company discovered tampering with the personal identification number (PIN) pads at its checkout lanes in stores across 20 States.
- In August 2006, two circulation pumps at Unit 3 of the Browns Ferry, Alabama, nuclear power plant failed, forcing the unit to be shut down manually. The failure of the pumps was traced to excessive traffic on the control system network, possibly caused by the failure of another control system device.

These incidents illustrate the serious impact that cyber threats can have on Federal agency operations, the operations of critical infrastructures, and the security of sensitive personal and financial information.

In summary, the cyber threats facing the Nation are evolving and growing, with a wide array of potential threat actors having access to increasingly sophisticated techniques for exploiting system vulnerabilities. The danger posed by these threats is heightened by the weaknesses that continue to exist in Federal information systems and systems supporting critical infrastructures. Ensuring the security of these systems is critical to avoiding potentially devastating impacts, including loss, disclosure, or modification of personal or sensitive information; disruption or destruction of critical infrastructure; and damage to our National and economic security.

Chairman McCaul, Ranking Member Keating, and Members of the subcommittee, this concludes my statement. I would be happy to answer any questions you have at this time.

Mr. McCaul. Thank you for your testimony.
The Chairman now recognizes Mr. McClure.

STATEMENT OF STUART MC CLURE, CHIEF TECHNOLOGY OFFICER, MC AFEE

Mr. McClure. Thank you Chairman, thank you Members. So . . . I am the global CTO for McAfee. Ultimately I am responsible for all the technology that comes out of the company and all the protective measures that we put in place. But I also used to run the labs within McAfee. The labs are responsible for all malware that comes in and a quick turnaround to protect our customers.

Now, when I was running the labs, it was probably about 2005–2006, we had upwards of about maybe 1,000 samples every single day that came into our networks that we had to go and respond to and build signatures and countermeasures for. Today we receive 80,000 that must be responded to. These are unique, these are malicious, and they are something that we have to find protective countermeasures to.

This is a huge exponential problem that we have. If I had a blank check to write to hire as many people as I wanted, to put as many controls in place as I wanted, I could not do it to respond to all of these threats. It is a huge, huge problem.

Another part of my background, I also wrote a very successful computer security book called "Hacking Exposed." The whole point behind the book was to expose how the hacker thinks, how the hacker works and achieves its primary goals and targets, and leaves very stealthily. That book has been very successful in helping administrators understand, and ITs as well, to understand how they work, because I do, really, believe passionately that if you cannot understand how they work, you will never be able to prevent them effectively. We are starting to see that today.

Now, one thing I wanted to share with you is so many years ago we used to talk mostly amongst us—I have been doing this a long time, about 20-plus years—and we would say, well, at least this cyber thing has not gotten to the physical world, it can't really kill anybody. That was the idea. So we got to put our heads down on the pillows and actually feel pretty good about that.

But I can tell you right now, definitively, I can personally kill somebody with my computer. I have already demonstrated this potential many times, and it is something that I want to make sure I get across, that the link between cyber and physical is here.

Now, I am—the demo that I have done in the past has been around, a particular insulin pump, okay, but it proves the point, which is that given no connection to this particular pump, I can overdose, okay, the insulin that is in there. This is just indicative of the bigger and broader problem.

It became really personal for me when my friend, who is a diabetic and has the exact pump, I asked him, hey, can I borrow your pump real quick, I am just going to test it out, you know, trust me, there is no problem here. He would not do it, he was freaked out. He flat refused, and to be honest I think it compromised a friendship in a way. But it drove home the point for me, which is this stuff, the technology that helps people either in biomed or otherwise protects and keeps people alive. So it is something to think about as we go forward.

Now, we always talk about the threats basically in three areas: Motivation, opportunity, and ability. Of course you have heard a lot about the motivation, financial, ego-driven, hacktivism, purpose, you name it, we see it all the time. Opportunity. The big problem in this formula is the opportunity. There are so many opportunities. The number of devices are just exploding out there, and they are all interconnected 24/7, everything from your mobile devices to tablets to insulin pumps to critical infrastructure for that matter. Also the vulnerabilities that are present on them are growing all the time, and that is the core of the problem, these vulnerabilities on the assets. The ability is only getting better.

So every day, more and more people get smarter and smarter, the tool kits get easier and easier to download and buy on-line. It is those variables in that formula are the big problem, and they are not going anywhere but up. So what we have to do is think about it, I think, in a better way. So information sharing is absolutely critical and key. I have been talking about that for a long time. We have to be able to share that valuable data. We can clear the privacy issues. I really—I believe that it doesn't take much to allow the critical data to be shared effectively in a timely manner.

But the other part that we have to think about is security by design. This is the big problem. We develop software, we develop hardware, and quite frankly no one—very, very few think about security in that design process and in the planning. It is that process that we have to try to instill in the coming years to truly affect the core problem; otherwise, all we are doing is affecting the symptoms. It would be like taking a decongestant or a pain reliever when you have a cold, rather than eating healthy and exercising and building your immunity.

So with that, I want to say thank you very much for your time.

[The prepared statement of Mr. McClure follows:]

PREPARED STATEMENT OF STUART MCCLURE

APRIL 24, 2012

Good afternoon Chairman McCaul, Ranking Member Keating, and other Members of the subcommittee. I am Stuart McClure, Executive Vice President and Worldwide Chief Technology Officer for McAfee. Thank you for requesting my views on this important topic.

You asked me to focus on the cyber threat, so my testimony will focus on threats to consumers, to intellectual property, and to critical infrastructure. During my discussion I will attempt to highlight the following points:
- The world's continual drive to innovate has driven unprecedented connectivity which has given rise to exploding numbers of cyber threats and attacks.
- The only way to definitively solve this problem—and it is solvable—is through "security by design."
- There are policy initiatives, such as enhanced information sharing and other measures, that would dramatically help respond to these threats.

First I would like to provide some background on my professional experience and on McAfee.

As Global CTO, I work closely with senior leaders at McAfee to ensure strong collaboration on customer requirements, knowledge sharing, strategy, development efforts, advanced threat research, and technology patents. Prior to joining McAfee, I held positions as executive director of security services for Kaiser Permanente, a $34 billion health care organization; served as senior vice president of global threats and research at McAfee Labs, where I led an elite global security threats team; and was founder, president, and chief technology officer of Foundstone, which was acquired by McAfee in 2004.

I have dedicated my entire professional life to the practice of cybersecurity. My first book, *Hacking Exposed,* was published in 1999 and has been translated into more than 30 languages and has become the definitive best-selling computer security book teaching the good guys how the bad guys think and attack. I have demonstrated literally hundreds of hacker techniques in front of live audiences for the better part of 20 years, as I believe a picture is worth a 1,000 words and a demo is worth millions.

MCAFEE'S ROLE IN CYBERSECURITY

McAfee, Inc. protects businesses, consumers, and the Government/public sector from cyber-attacks, viruses, and a wide range of on-line security threats. Headquartered in Santa Clara, California, and Plano, Texas, McAfee is the world's largest dedicated security technology company and is a proven force in combating the world's toughest security challenges. McAfee is a wholly-owned subsidiary of Intel Corporation.

McAfee delivers proactive and proven solutions, services, and global threat intelligence that help secure systems and networks around the world, allowing users to safely connect to the internet and browse and shop the web more securely. Fueled by an award-winning research team, McAfee creates innovative products that empower home users, businesses, the public sector, and service providers by enabling them to prove compliance with regulations, protect data, prevent disruptions, identify vulnerabilities, and continuously monitor and improve their security.

To help organizations take full advantage of their security infrastructure, McAfee launched the Security Innovation Alliance, which brings together more than 150 partners, large and small, to allow organizations access into our extensible management platform and thereby detect and prevent attacks in real time.

THE DOUBLE EDGE OF CONNECTIVITY

Today, we are always on and always connected. The world of instantaneous communication and constant connectivity we have come to take for granted is limited only by our powers of creativity and innovation—and those seem to have no end. For years policymakers have heard of the numerous benefits that this interconnected, always-on world can and does bring to the areas of education, health and medicine, energy, and transportation, as well as to individual well-being and the American economy at large. Indeed, the Federal Communications Commission has now redefined "universal service" from a program designed to create universal telephone service, to a program that will create Nation-wide high-speed broadband access. There is no turning back from this path, nor should we want to.

The reality, however, is that this same world of connectivity also creates risk. Risk is dictated by three factors: Opportunity, motivation, and ability. If you are able to affect any one or more of these factors, you reduce the overall risk. In today's environment, all three factors—opportunity, motivation, and ability—are growing inordinately.

Let me start with motivation. By now you have heard much about a variety of criminal actors who are highly motivated—either by money, National pride, religion, or some other compelling factor. These actors have huge amounts to gain with hardly anything to lose; our laws and penalties, in addition to our inability to enforce them, make cyber crime extremely attractive and profitable. There are few real deterrents to cyber crime and there is much to gain.

Add to this the fact that the level of ability of most cyber criminals has increased dramatically from the days of the pimply teenager working out of his garage. Now there are serious professionals and even companies for hire. Simply put, attacks are relatively easy to perform, leveraging thousands and even millions of computers to attack a single target, creating virtual armies that are far less expensive and more dynamic than physical armies. The tools and techniques are well-documented, easy to find, and the range of a malicious individual armed with a laptop and an internet connection surpasses that of any ICBM.

Who has the opportunity? Certainly insiders—those with knowledge of the organization and its most sensitive data and systems—have optimum opportunity. But in the highly interconnected world, a cyber attacker certainly does not have to BE inside an organization to GET inside it. Indeed, almost any device that we use regularly—mobile phone, tablet, laptop, thumb drive, automobile, and even a medical device—is perfectly capable of letting an attacker inside. Anything that you can connect to, or that can be connected to—through USB, wired network connection, WiFi network connection, Bluetooth, RFID—is enough to let a cyber criminal in.

Yet the other great reality about a world that is becoming increasingly interconnected is the degree to which connected devices are helping individuals address significant challenges, and many of these challenges are highly personal. For example, diabetics can now use insulin pumps that are connected wirelessly; homeowners can set their burglar alarm or control the temperature of their homes remotely; patients with heart conditions can stay home while doctors monitor their conditions from their offices; students in rural areas can take classes at major universities; motorists can have their car's door locks unlocked from remote or be routed to their exact destination and soon might be able to drive on smart highways.

This list is by no means exhaustive. Innovative companies have every incentive to offer more and more goods and services addressing the most fundamental needs of consumers while at the same time make them more interconnected. This is a powerful market trend that will continue in the future. But unless the devices are locked down and secured by design, the cyber criminals will be given even more opportunities to profit, plunder, and pillage.

THE RISK TO INDIVIDUALS AND CONSUMERS

Most consumers expect that when they go on-line, they will be safe, their information will be private, and their kids will be protected as long as they do not go on websites from which their parents have barred them. But this is an illusion. For every control, there is a bypass.

The threats that individuals and consumers face run the gamut from identity theft to loss of financial or personal information, to infection of their systems and destruction of hardware, software, and data. The advent of new mobile technology, particularly smartphones and tablets, has opened up new attack vectors for hackers.

According to a recent House Science Committee witness from Idaho National Labs, Dr. Rangam Subramanian, every key economic sector will soon be dependent on wireless: Energy and power, public safety, finance, health care, transportation, entertainment, and more. Yet for all the convenience and innovation that wireless brings, it also introduces even more opportunities for hackers.

Many Americans now engage in personal banking, shopping, and other services by accessing Wi-Fi hot spots on their smartphones, which can lead them directly into traps set by cyber criminals. And the wireless revolution is only in its infancy. Cisco's U.S. mobile data forecast projects that mobile data traffic will increase 16 times from 2011 to 2016 for a compound annual growth rate of 74 percent. By 2016, mobile data traffic will be equivalent to four times the volume of the entire U.S. internet in 2005. The United States is a leader in the area of wireless innovation, and it is to our National advantage to have that leadership continue. The key is to ensure that that innovation incorporates security by design.

Following are just some of the most recent threats to consumers:

Social networking sites.—The social networking phenomenon has overtaken pornography as the No. 1 internet activity and has brought traditionally non-computer savvy users onto the internet in droves. As an example, if Facebook were a country, it would be the 3rd largest in the world with over 850 million users. And cyber criminals know this. The attack surface area is large, but they might, for example, send what appears to be a harmless video but when clicked on it downloads a malicious virus.

Mobile devices.—While PCs remain the bigger targets, smartphones—which of course are miniature, mobile computers—are quickly capturing cyber criminals' attention, with instances of mobile malware increasing by 600% from 2010 to 2011. McAfee Labs again saw the Android platform firmly ensconced as the No. 1 target for writers of mobile malware. However, it is a misconception that Mac platforms are invulnerable to attack. As Apple recently learned with the Flashback Trojan, even their MacBooks can be victims, with over 600,000 infections to date. The hackers go where the numbers are, and the more ubiquitous iPhones and iPads become, the more they will be targeted by hackers.

Mobile apps.—In 2011, apps that appeared legitimate were bundled with malware and distributed over Google's Android Marketplace. Google was able to remotely detect and delete more than 50 infected applications from thousands of Android devices. Every day, consumers download apps from unknown apps stores without a second thought. We advise consumers to download apps only from well-known, reputable app stores, check reviews and apps ratings before downloading them, read the fine print to check what permissions the app is accessing, and install a comprehensive mobile security product, including those from McAfee or other vendors.

Phishing scams and IRS scams.—During the tax season, in particular, hackers are known to conduct scams that involved phishing—a way of attempting to acquire information such as usernames, passwords, and credit card details by masquerading as a trustworthy entity. Some criminal actors masquerade as the IRS or an entity closely related to the IRS. We advise consumers never to respond to or click on links within unsolicited emails requesting that they enter personal data or visit a website to update account information—especially from the IRS, as they do not send out emails to consumers.

Perhaps one of the most unsettling examples of individuals being exposed to cyber attacks on a personal level entails the use of personal medical devices. Recently a McAfee researcher identified a security flaw in a wirelessly-enabled insulin pump, which allows the device to be controlled by a hacker and subsequently administer a potentially lethal dose of insulin to diabetes patients. While there are several security holes in the device, the principal vulnerability comes from the wireless connection between the glucose monitoring system and the pump itself, which is vital to determining how much insulin is dispensed.

Since that story was publicized, I've heard from several friends who either used the pump in question themselves or whose child did. When they asked me if their pumps—and thus their lives—were vulnerable to cyber attack, I had to answer "yes." Again, medical device manufacturers are making great strides in reducing inconvenience for individuals, yet at what price? Unless devices are built from the ground up with security by design, the price could be high.

Another example is automobiles. Many security researchers have noticed an alarming number of vectors of attack inside today's increasingly computerized cars. They have discovered that cars are as insecure as PCs were some 20 years ago, fraught with ways into the system and vulnerabilities to attack. In fact, researchers from the University of Washington and the University of California, San Diego, have released findings over the past 2 years detailing how they could not only open a locked car without the keys but they could remotely penetrate a car's IVI (in-vehicle infotainment) system to then take over control of much of the car's features, including disabling airbag and brakes. Both these examples show that in our highly interconnected world, you don't have to be sitting at a computer or holding a smartphone to be vulnerable to cyber attack.

THE RISK TO INTELLECTUAL PROPERTY

One of the most insidious types of threats to individuals, corporations, organizations, Government agencies, and the economy as a whole is the theft of intellectual property. Today, malware developers combine web, host, and network vulnerabilities with spam, rootkits (invisible malware that hides within authorized software in a computer's operating system), spyware, worms (which target computers rather than software programs but which can clog communications bandwidth and overload computers or networks,) and other means of attack. Malware also can be distributed indirectly by networks of computers that have been corrupted by a criminal—known as a "botnet," or a collection of compromised computers connected to the internet.

Then there is the type of attack known as an Advanced Persistent Threat (APT), which has received much attention recently. The APT is essentially an insidious, persistent intruder meant to fly below the radar screen and quietly explore and steal the contents of the target network.

In the past 3 years, McAfee has uncovered numerous APTs affecting tens of thousands of organizations worldwide. These attacks are significant because they were managed by well-coordinated, organized teams that succeeded in extracting billions of dollars of intellectual property from leading global companies in the information technology, defense, and energy sectors—strategic industries vital to any country's long-term economic success and National security. These low-profile attacks are often more dangerous than high-profile incursions because they are a type of cyber espionage, providing silent, on-going access to protected institutional information. And these APTs are not limited in scope; they can affect any company, government body, or nation, regardless of sector, size, or geography.

However, as the United States is the largest producer of intellectual property in the world, we are an especially rich target. The onslaught of increasingly sophisticated targeted attacks is reflected in growing information breach statistics. A 2010 survey found that 60 percent of organizations report a "chronic and recurring loss" of sensitive information. The average cost of a data breach reached $7.2 million in 2010 and cost companies $214 per compromised data record, according to the Ponemon Institute. And that's just the cost to respond internally to a data breach. If a company's intellectual property is stolen, it could decimate an organization.

We do not have statistics for all of the IP breached, as organizations can be reluctant to report IP theft, fearing that it will cause customers and markets to lose confidence. Again, by building products and systems that are secure from the ground up, these fears, costs, and substantial drain of American competitive innovation could be greatly reduced.

THE RISK TO CRITICAL SYSTEMS AND INFRASTRUCTURE

As policymakers have begun to recognize, a cyber attack—or series of cyber attacks—to the Nation's critical infrastructure could be tremendously devastating to our way of life. Let's take the electrical grid, by far the most vulnerable of our critical infrastructures.

Almost every aspect of American life depends on electricity—from producing goods to saving lives, from defending the country to conducting electronic banking and commerce, from simple communications to feeding our families safely. Yet the systems used to manage our electricity, the supervisory control and data acquisition, or SCADA systems, are antiquated, running on commonly available operating systems, and with their design having changed little since their introduction decades ago. They were never designed or built securely, and they certainly were not meant to be connected to the internet. And even today, we find that many electric companies still use vendor-supplied default passwords because they allow easy access in times of crisis or for maintenance and repair.

A report by CSIS and McAfee interviewing executives in the energy and power sector found that a large majority of them had reported cyber attacks, and about 55% of these attacks targeted SCADA. In 2009, nearly half of the respondents said that they had never faced large-scale denial of service attacks or network infiltrations. By 2010, those numbers had changed dramatically; 80 percent had faced a large-scale denial-of-service attack, and 85 percent had experienced network infiltrations. Meanwhile, a quarter of the interviewees reported daily or weekly denial-of-service attacks on a large scale. A similar number reported that they had been the victim of extortion through network attacks or the threat of network attacks. Nearly two-thirds reported they frequently (at least monthly) found malware designed for sabotage on their system.

Attacks on systems like SCADA can give hackers direct control of operational systems, creating the potential for large-scale power outages or man-made environmental disasters. Yet in the United States, many companies have not adopted security measures for their SCADA systems, and many report their SCADA systems connected to IP networks or the internet, making these systems even more susceptible to attacks.

What happens when there are multiple, simultaneous failures or system manipulations in the electric grid? Industry experts acknowledge that the grid is not currently equipped to handle this situation. While the experts say that the odds of a natural event or a physical attack creating this situation have been quite low, they are not prepared to say that for cyber—which all agree is the threat most likely to give rise to this kind of power failure.

What could happen? Imagine that cyber criminals have been gaining access to various parts of the power grid for years. They have infiltrated enough systems to make it possible to knock out power for the entire Northeast grid. They launch an attack in winter and power goes down throughout the area. Not only do people lose heat, light, refrigeration, cooking facilities, communication, and entertainment, but the systems that pump our water from reservoirs—and those that purify the water in the reservoirs—are affected. No potable water, perhaps no water at all, and no capacities for managing sewage.

Even if stores have back-up generators, they cannot order the inventory because their systems are electronic. Banking comes to a halt because funds can no longer move electronically. Gas stations can no longer sell gasoline. Commerce effectively ends because order fulfillment systems are down, payment systems are down, and communication is down. Those consumers with phone service through the internet—including those triple play plans offered by major providers—are out of luck because their service is no longer over the traditional land-line telephone network. Hospitals and medical centers, which might also have independent generators, can care for only the most critical patients, as they cannot check on patients' insurance status or connect with the outside world electronically. While many of these sectors have emergency back-up systems to enable them to maintain operations during a power failure, those back-up systems are meant to be temporary—not long-term.

I personally experienced something like this as a child living on the island of Guam. A devastating and powerful typhoon knocked out power for many weeks and we had to run back and forth between the slowly moving water truck driving down the street and the house's bathtub where we emptied the bucket and ran back. The memory of that time is vivid, but it was not nearly as bad as it might have been had the situation gone on longer.

SECURITY BY DESIGN

Adding security features into systems after they have been developed is a losing battle. Remember the sunroof of the 1980's? The only way to get one was to get it installed aftermarket. Manufacturers did not offer one as an option on new cars. And many of them leaked badly. Today, every manufacturer offers a sunroof as an option to your new car—and they never leak!

Cybersecurity has to be the same: It must be baked into the equipment, systems, and networks at the very start of the design process. Security must be intrinsic to an organization's thought processes, its business processes, and its design, development, and manufacturing processes. It must be embedded in a product or network element so that it becomes an integral part of the product's or element's functioning. This approach is not only more effective; it is less cumbersome and less expensive than trying to lock down systems that are inherently insecure.

POLICY RECOMMENDATIONS

Given the level of the cybersecurity threat, the Government has a legitimate interest in ensuring that our country is protected from cyber attacks. The first order of business must be for the Government to fully protect its own institutions, and we support rapid passage of FISMA reform legislation. The Government also has an obligation to work with our companies and citizens to improve the level of security at work and in the home. I believe that positive incentives are superior to regulation in achieving the desired National outcome: A cyber-secure Nation. Using positive incentives rather than negative ones, such as Government mandates, is the most effective way to drive higher levels of trust and actual cooperation between the private sector and Government—all vital to producing real success. Having the private sector fully commit—customers and vendors of IT products and services—to the principles and implementation of security by design will do much to help make our country more secure in the future.

There are a variety of legislative approaches focused on positive incentives in play right now that I believe can make a major contribution to addressing our country's cybersecurity challenges. Many of the recommendations of Representative Thornberry's (R–Texas) Cybersecurity Task Force are a step in the right direction in that they address a wide range of incentives such as information sharing, insurance reforms, and tax credits. And over the past few years there has been good bipartisan collaboration on a number of cyber initiatives, including additional investment in cybersecurity research and FISMA reform, to name just a few.

In this same spirit, better information sharing would be particularly effective in encouraging the kind of public-private partnerships we need to move forward in cybersecurity. There have been several proposed Government solutions, and many of them share McAfee's goal that Government facilitate collaboration and encourage trusted working relationships to the benefit of all parties in the internet ecosystem.

Better enabling information sharing is critical for addressing the cyber threat. This would help organizations execute with the alacrity shown by our cyber adversaries, as previously described. There are also other positive incentives that can help address some of our Nation's fundamental challenges—challenges in hiring the right type of cybersecurity experts, regulatory disincentives, economic disincentives, and the immaturity of the insurance market, which has limited the growth of the kind of insurance programs needed for companies to insure against catastrophic losses:

- *Litigation/Legal Reform.*—Imposing limitations on liability for damages as well as for non-economic losses would remove a serious obstacle to information security investments—i.e., the risk of losses for which responsibility is assigned notwithstanding a company's good faith investments in adequate information security. Eliminating that risk, at least for companies that meet high, "best practices" security standards, would encourage more security on a company-by-company basis. This approach can help create positive incentives for disclosure through liability relief for responsible organizations to improve the Nation's overall cybersecurity posture.
- *Competitions, Scholarships, and Research and Development Funding.*—Cybersecurity competitions and challenges, as well as scholarship and creativity to programs, can help identify and recruit talented individuals to the field to augment the future cybersecurity workforce. Similarly, research and development grants foster innovation and advance basic and applied solutions. Recognizing this, several legislative proposals under consideration contain provisions designed to help industry meet the cybersecurity challenges of tomorrow and train the next generation of experts.
- *Tax Incentives.*—Accelerated depreciation or refundable tax credits are being considered to encourage critical infrastructure industries to make additional investments in cybersecurity technologies, solutions, and human capital. The same approaches could be effectively applied to small businesses. Despite the current environment where balancing the budget is a critical priority, we cannot afford to be shortsighted. Cybersecurity-related tax incentives would prove to be a legitimate, long-term investment in security that would protect our National security and economic interests.
- *Insurance Reforms.*—Many companies defer investments in improved security out of a concern that, even with improved security, they are not protected from liability for losses that occur. Similarly, insurance carriers are reluctant to create a vigorous marketplace for cybersecurity insurance, thereby hindering investment. Government should give consideration to implementing reinsurance programs to help underwrite the development of cybersecurity insurance programs. Over time, these reinsurance programs could be phased out as insurance markets gained experience with cybersecurity coverage.

CONCLUSION

As Global CTO for the world's largest dedicated security company, I carry a heavy burden, but one to which I have dedicated my entire career: To protect the world from cybersecurity attacks. But I stay focused on this task because I believe I can make a difference to provide a safer world for our children.

Thank you for giving me the opportunity to take part in this hearing on behalf of McAfee. The cybersecurity challenge faced by our country is a serious matter that requires an evolution in the way in which both the public and private sectors collaborate. Each sector has its own set of core capabilities. Only the Government can implement the complex set of organizational and policy responses necessary to counter the growing cybersecurity threat. Leading information technology companies and their customers are uniquely positioned to act as early warning systems that can identify and help address cybersecurity attacks. Information technology companies focused on cybersecurity, in particular, have the resources and the economic incentives to continue to invent and develop the technologies and solutions needed to stay ahead of sophisticated cyber attackers. Aligning Government incentives with a National objective of achieving security by design in all of our systems is consistent with the best American tradition of collaboration. The public and private sectors have made important strides to address the cybersecurity challenge. As we work together to further evolve our collaboration models, we can succeed in protecting our homeland from the threat of cyber attacks.

Mr. McCAUL. Thank you Mr. McClure. I agree with you that I think we have made the jump from virtual to physical as well.

With that, the Chairman recognizes Dr. Flynn for his testimony.

STATEMENT OF STEPHEN E. FLYNN, FOUNDING CO-DIREC-TOR, GEORGE J. KOSTAS RESEARCH INSTITUTE FOR HOME-LAND SECURITY, NORTHEASTERN UNIVERSITY

Mr. FLYNN. Thank you very much Mr. Chairman, Ranking Member Keating, Ranking Member Thompson. It is an honor to be before you all, distinguished Members of the subcommittee. I would like to build on the conversation we have had already today, the testimony we have already had today, and essentially assign an explanation point I think to the risk.

As I see it, this subcommittee certainly well understands the serious nature of the challenge, but we really have as a country not stepped up to this risk.

I want to share with you a scenario that was actually developed by the National Institute of Standards and Technology, the NIST, in an attack on the U.S. electric grid to kind of drive home the stakes involved with this. According to the NIST study, they provide the following scenario. Using war dialers, simple computer programs that dial consecutive phone numbers looking for modems, an adversary finds modems connected to programmable breakers of the electric power transmission control systems, they crack the passwords that control access to the breakers and change the control settings to cause local power outages and damage equipment. The adversary lowers the settings from 500 amps to 200 amps on some circuit breakers, taking those lines out of service, and then diverting power to neighboring lines. At the same time the adversary raises the settings on the neighboring lines to 900 amps which prevents the circuit breakers from tripping, plus overloading the lines. This causes significant damage to transformers and other critical equipment, resulting in lengthy repair outages.

This is not a particularly sophisticated attack and it can be carried out remotely by anybody with anonymity. The harm it could cause will be far beyond the disruption of service and the loss of data. When you can successfully disable a portion of the power grid, you can generate cascading consequences. When transformers fail, so too will water distribution, waste management, transportation, communications, and many emergency Government services. People who take medicines that require refrigeration will quickly face the prospect of going without those drugs.

Given the average of a 12-month lead that is required to replace a damaged transformer today with a new one if we had a mass

damage of that scale in a local regional level, the economic and societal disruption would be enormous.

There are lots of potential target or opportunity, as Mr. McClure
laid out. We have a power grid that operates with 5,300 power
plants that, combined, produce 1,075 gigawatts that is moved from
power plants to 140 homes and businesses via 211 miles of high-
voltage transmission lines and thousands of substations.

Again, the cyber world and the physical world is here. The things
that we are talking about messing with are things that we rely on
and largely take for granted. The issue is primarily that these attacks can go after the industrial control systems that are central
to their operation. As these vulnerable industrial control systems
are used remotely to manage everything from waste, water, oil
pipelines, refineries, and power generation plants, transportation
systems, mass transit to maritime port operations, an attack on
these systems can produce not only a catastrophic disruption, but
destruction, loss of life. Here we really need to wake up and recognize that we have a problem that hackers cannot only break into
systems but take control of them. Doing things like turning off
alarms or sending bad data to falsely trigger alarms can essentially
cause the kind of mischief we just heard Mr. McClure can do with
an insulin device.

So, given this urgency, flashing back to my own career in the
Coast Guard, the model should be "all hands on deck." But I would
argue that to date, American universities and academic institutions
have been largely left on the sidelines. We talk about private-pub-
lic, but we fail to engage the various institutions that are involved
in developing so many of these technologies and developing the culture which we have to operate in, for better or for worse. Universities, I would argue, can play a key role in helping us to move forward in the face of this risk. They can offer expertise to play an
honest broker role between the private and public sectors. Universities can bridge that expertise and trust gap by its convening of
power and offering technical advice where it can be helpful. They
also can—another point Mr. McClure just made, the importance of
baking in cybersecurity. Universities have been and will continue
to be the incubators for information technology and applications.
The time for thinking about incorporating safeguards is when they
are under development, not after they are being widely used by
consumers and industry. When security measures are an afterthought, they often end up being costly and suboptimal.

Developing and maintaining standards that can mitigate cyber
threats, vulnerabilities, and consequences and help to sustain or
rapidly recover central functions and trust, needs to become an organic part of critical infrastructures, systems, and networks. Academic institutions need to be made an active partner in that effort.

Finally, the need to develop a culture of cybersecurity. At the end
of the day, we are going to need young people involved with this,
and we have got a lot of them in the academic and university
world. We should go there to try to get them involved, to be part
of the solution, not potentially be a part of the problem.

In conclusion, I would like to recommend to the committee to
consider really actively embracing some of the proposed legislation
that Ranking Member Keating has been advancing to advance re-

gional university-based cybersecurity research centers ideally located in several places in part of the country. We need to mobilize civil society, we need to mobilize intellectual capital we have in this country to address this very urgent problem.

Thank you very much Mr. Chairman.

[The prepared statement of Mr. Flynn follows:]

PREPARED STATEMENT OF STEPHEN E. FLYNN

APRIL 24, 2012

Chairman McCaul, Ranking Member Keating, distinguished Members of the subcommittee, thank you for the opportunity to testify about the serious and growing cybersecurity threat facing consumers, industry, and government at all levels in the United States. The significant vulnerability of critical infrastructure such as the electric grid and transportation infrastructure, information and financial systems, and everyday American consumers to cyber threats is why today's hearing is so timely and why urgent action by Congress is so needed.

My name is Stephen Flynn. I am the founding Co-Director of the Kostas Research Institute for Homeland Security and professor of Political Science at Northeastern University in Boston, Massachusetts. I am also a member of the Homeland Security Project at the Bipartisan Policy Center that is led by 9/11 Commission co-chairs Governor Tom Kean and Congressman Lee Hamilton. The Nation's exposure to a growing array of cybersecurity threats is one of deep concern to the co-chairs and all the members of our group of distinguished National security and homeland security leaders.

At the Kostas Institute, our mission is to help advance resilience in the face of 21st Century risks so that America can better withstand, nimbly respond, rapidly recover, and adapt to man-made and natural disruptions. As such, we are working with our Northeastern colleagues in the College of Computer & Information Science, College of Engineering, and College of Social Sciences and Humanities to make cybersecurity a primary area of focus. We are a particularly interested in better safeguarding industrial control systems that are key to the operation of much of the Nation's critical physical infrastructure.

The Kostas Institute is housed in a new 70,000-square-foot research facility located in the heart of the metro-Boston high-technology corridor where it provides a secure environment for innovative translational research conducted by private-public-academic multidisciplinary research teams. Northeastern is also home to the Institute for Information Assurance, which is one of the National Security Agency's (NSA) Centers of Excellence. In addition, the university is a member, along with MIT, Harvard, Boston University, and the University of Massachusetts, of the Advanced Cyber Security Center hosted at the MITRE Corporation in Bedford, Massachusetts. Given the historic leadership role that Northeastern, our neighboring universities, and the information technology industry that is concentrated in the metro-Boston area have played in high-tech development, we feel a special responsibility to help manage, stem, and mitigate the growing risks to critical systems from cyber threats. To this end, we are committed to bringing together expert researchers and practitioners to identify risks and their potential consequences, to develop next-generation secure applications and computing architecture, and to promote best practices with our counterparts around the United States and globally.

NATURE OF THE CYBERSECURITY THREAT

The cybersecurity threat is one of the most serious economic and National security challenges we face as a Nation. Quite simply, the United States is at risk of becoming a victim of its own success. Our position as the world's dominant economic power can be attributed in no small part to the speed at which Americans have developed and embraced information technology systems and applications. But while we have been leading and benefiting from the information age, there has been too little consideration to the security implications of our growing reliance on information technologies.

A particularly worrisome vulnerability is the extent to which over the past decade, more and more Internet Protocol (IP) devices have been replacing proprietary hardware, software, and communications protocols for the Nation's physical infrastructure. As industrial control systems (ICS) become increasingly accessible to the Internet, cyber attacks can be launched at the electrical power grid; water and waste management systems; oil pipelines, refineries, and power-generation plants; and transportation systems ranging from mass-transit to maritime port operations. An attack on these systems by a state or non-state actor, not only places at risk the continuity of service or the compromise of databases, but the potential for catastrophic loss of life and destruction of property. This is because computer hackers are not only able to infiltrate systems, but they are increasingly in a position to actually take control of such systems—turning off alarms or sending bad data that falsely triggers an alarm. Unfortunately, bad actors need not be terribly sophisticated in order to accomplish substantial harm. Because of the interconnectivity of our networks, successful disabling of just one critical system can generate cascading consequences across multiple systems.

The U.S. power grid is particularly vulnerable to the risk of cyber attacks and given the reliance on power by all other sectors, it deserves special and urgent attention. As with other large and disbursed infrastructures that make up America's critical industrial landscape, managing the electric grid depends on the operation of supervisory control and data acquisition (SCADA) systems and distributed control systems (DCS). SCADA systems make it possible to control geographically dispersed assets remotely by acquiring status data and monitoring alarms. Based on the information received from the remote station control devices, automatic or operator-driven supervisory commands can be provided from a centralized location. These field devices can perform such functions as opening and closing breakers and operating the speed of motors based on the data received from sensor systems. Distributed control systems (DCS) are typically facility-centric and used to control localized industrial processes such as the flow of steam into turbines to support generation of power in an electric plant. DCS and SCADA systems are networked together so that the operation of a power generation facility can be well-coordinated with the demand for transmission and distribution.[1]

When most industrial control systems (ICS) were originally installed to help operate components of the power grid, they relied on logic functions that were executed by electrical hardware such as relays, switches, and mechanical timers. Security generally involved physically protecting access to the consoles that controlled the system. But, over time, microprocessors, personal computers, and networking technologies were incorporated into ICS designs. Then in the late 1990's, more and more Internet Protocol (IP) devices were embraced so as to allow managers to gain better access to real-time systems data on their corporate networks. These networks are, in turn, often connected to the internet. The inevitable result of this increased reliance on standard computers and operating systems is to make ICS more vulnerable to computer hackers.[2]

Tampering with DCS and SCADA systems can have serious personal safety consequences since industrial control systems directly control assets in the physical world. According to a June 2011 report by the National Institute of Standards and Technology (NIST), cybersecurity breaches of industrial control systems could include unauthorized changes to the instructions, commands, or alarm thresholds that result in disabling, damaging, or shutting down key components. Alternatively, false information about the status of systems can be sent that cause human operators to make adjustments or to take emergency actions that inadvertently cause harm. If a cyber attack leads to a power-generating unit being taken off-line because of the loss of monitoring and control capabilities, it could result in a loss of power to a transmission substation, triggering failures across the power grid if other substations are not able to carry the added load. The resultant blackouts would affect oil and natural gas production, water treatment facilities, wastewater collection systems, refinery operations, and pipeline transport systems.[3]

---

[1] U.S. Department of Commerce. Guide to Industrial Control Systems (ICS) Security, (Special Publication 800–82, Jun. 2011) by K. Stouffer, J. Falco and K. Scarfone.
[2] Ibid.
[3] Ibid.

41

POTENTIAL CASCADING EFFECTS OF ELECTRIC POWER FAILURE

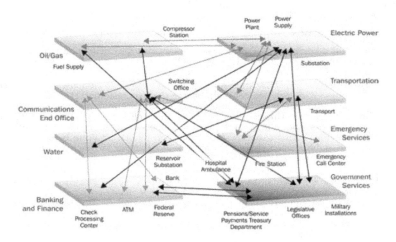

Source: Department of Homeland Security.[4]

A possible scenario hypothesized by the NIST is illustrative:

Using war dialers—simple computer programs that dial consecutive phone numbers looking for modems—an adversary finds modems connected to the programmable breakers of the electric power transmission control system, cracks the passwords that control access to the breakers, and changes the control settings to cause local power outages and damage equipment. The adversary lowers the settings from 500 Ampere (A) to 200 A on some circuit breakers, taking those lines out of service and diverting power to neighboring lines. At the same time, the adversary raises the settings on neighboring lines to 900 A, preventing the circuit breakers from tripping, thus overloading the lines. This causes significant damage to transformers and other critical equipment, resulting in lengthy repair outages.[5]

When transformers fail, so too will water distribution, transportation, communications, and many emergency and Government services. Given the 12-month lead time typically required to replace a damaged transformer with a new one,[6] the local and regional economic and societal disruption caused by a cyber attacks that that disable or destroy the mechanical functioning of key components of the power grid would be devastating.

Beyond this exposure of long-standing industrial infrastructure to cyber threats, there is a serious risk to the emerging computing environment as well. As mobile devices, from smart phones to iPads have proliferated, so too has mobile malware reflecting the painful reality that security still receives insufficient attention by the private sector responsible for rushing to market new informational technology tools and applications. According to a March 2012 company survey conducted at a major IT conference, 68 percent of security professionals reported currently having no way of identifying known mobile device vulnerabilities that could be affecting their networks.[7] Mobile devices are being targeted to steal users' authentication credentials

---

[4] National Aeronautics and Space Administration. NASA Science News. Severe Space Weather—Social and Economic Impacts. June 2009 at *http://science.nasa.gov/science-news/science-at-nasa/2009/21jan_severespaceweather/*.

[5] U.S. Department of Commerce. Guide to Industrial Control Systems (ICS) Security, (Special Publication 800–82, Jun. 2011) by K. Stouffer, J. Falco and K. Scarfone. 3–17.

[6] National Aeronautics and Space Administration. NASA Science News. Solar Shield—Protecting the North American Power Grid. October 26, 2010 at *http://science.nasa.gov/sciencenews/science-at-nasa/2010/26oct_solarshield/*.

[7] "Mobile Device Vulnerability Management Flagged as Top Concern for Security Professionals in 2012," Press Release by Tenable Press Security (Apr 2, 2012) *http://finance.yahoo.com/news/mobile-device-vulnerability-management-flagged140900613.html*.

and financial information. Moreover, as new social networks emerge, users tend not to appreciate the permanent availability of data, which can facilitate hackers' identity theft and identity cloning efforts. It is these growing ubiquitous links on the internet that makes all Americans vulnerable to cyber threats that can damage very practical aspects of our lives.

THE CASE FOR MAKING UNIVERSITIES FULL-FLEDGED CYBER SECURITY PARTNERS

The potential contribution of American universities and academic institutions in advancing cybersecurity has been largely overlooked by the Executive Branch. There are three reasons why this oversight must be redressed.

(1) The need for expertise and for an honest broker to support public-private partnerships.—Universities can help bridge the expertise and trust gap between the public sector and private sector in developing standards, and—when appropriate—regulations. Universities can play this role by serving as neutral conveners between the public and private sectors and as arbiters of technical issues. Serving in this capacity should be seen as attractive to both the private sector and public sector, given the unique challenges for each associated with advancing cybersecurity.

The private sector, left largely on its own, has struggled to establish and enforce cybersecurity standards. In some instances this is because the information asymmetry associated with moral hazard; i.e., the developer of technologies and applications pass along risks because the costs will be disproportionately or wholly borne by the IT users that are attracted to the benefits of the tool, but lack an understanding of their resultant exposure to cyber threats and the associated consequences. There is also the tragedy of the commons dilemma arising from the fact that an entire system or network can be compromised by an attack on its weakest link. If compliance with a security standard is only voluntary, the vigilant company must worry that one or more of its competitors will find irresistible the temptation to forego the added cost of adopting the measure in a bid to boost market share or profits. As a result, the system remains vulnerable to disruption even if the vigilant company places itself at a competitive disadvantage by investing in the security measure.

The traditional way to deal with the problem associated with moral hazard and the tragedy of the commons dilemma is by adopting regulations that are well-enforced. But, effective regulations largely depend on the public sector having the requisite expertise to develop and oversee them. Unfortunately, in the case of cybersecurity, the Federal Government continues to face significant challenges with recruiting and retaining personnel with the appropriate technical background. This is particularly true of the Department of Homeland Security and other Federal agencies outside the Department of Defense, the National Security Agency, and the intelligence community.

Universities and the academic community should be enlisted to assist in addressing this deficit. Universities can help the private sector identify reasonable security options that can be embedded into critical infrastructures without causing undue disruption to dynamic and complex systems. Universities can also provide the public sector with the expertise that Government policy makers and officials need to keep up with the rapid pace and the growing complexity of information technologies and applications. Beyond the Office of University Programs within the DHS Science and Technology Directorate, Secretary Janet Napolitano has embraced the need for such coordination with the university community by recently establishing a Homeland Security Academic Advisory Council (HSAAC). HSAAC has been created so that the Department has a structured way to receive advice and input from university leaders who voluntary serve on the Council, including Northeastern University's President, Joseph E. Aoun. In 2011, Secretary Napolitano has also created an Office for Academic Engagement and appointed an Executive Director to serve within her office.

(2) The imperative to "bake-in" cybersecurity.—Universities have been and will continue to be incubators for information technology and applications. The time for thinking about incorporating safeguards is when they are under development, not after they are being widely used by consumers and industry. When security measures are an afterthought, they often end up being costly and suboptimal. Developing and maintaining standards that can mitigate cyber threats, vulnerabilities, and consequences, and help to sustain or rapidly recover essential functions and trust need to become an organic part of critical infrastruc-

tures, systems, and networks. Academic institutions need to be made an active partner in that effort.

(3) The need to develop a culture of cybersecurity.—Cybersecurity needs to be embedded in our information-age culture. Everyone needs to have a better understanding of cyber risks. This will require collaborative efforts that actively engage civil society, not just companies and Government agencies. There's no better way to develop this culture than by starting with young people who are attending academic institutions. An important way to advance this is to integrate cybersecurity within and across academic curriculums. Universities should be assigned a prominent role in conducting research, developing courses, and teaching as many informational technology users and providers as possible about the cyber dangers that we face and the security strategies and tactics that we need to embrace. The goal should be to create a new generation of students with the sophisticated skills to harness the opportunities of the information age without becoming victims of its dark side.

THE NEED FOR A COORDINATED RESEARCH & DEVELOPMENT STRATEGY

While pockets of knowledge exist about new and emerging cyber threats and the techniques for better safeguarding systems from attack, too many owners and operators of critical infrastructure continue to embrace information-age tools, including wireless and mobile devices, without adequately understanding the associated vulnerabilities and consequences. Faced with significant resource constraints, the Federal Government is largely trapped in the present, racing to respond to known threats to critical assets, often at the expense of developing the means to better anticipate new threats, to map out the associated risks, and to devise appropriate responses. There is also a National security imperative to develop offensive capabilities to deter or respond to attacks by state actors. It's in these areas that academic partners working together with industry and governments at all levels can be particularly helpful.

I applaud Chairman Dan Lungren and the efforts by Ranking Member Keating to introduce legislation that recognizes that preparing for and combatting cyber warfare requires robust academic, industry, and Federal research partnerships to design and implement secure systems for critical infrastructure. Yet, to date, the Nation's cybersecurity leaders have not yet fully engaged the academic research community in this effort. Meanwhile, industry is focused more on the near- and medium-term tasks of developing new products and applications. As the National Academies have noted, it largely falls to the Federal Government to play the indispensible role in sponsoring fundamental research that is key to developing the information technology talent that is used by industry and other parts of the economy. Chairman Lungren's proposed legislation appropriately recognizes the vital importance of a coordinated Federal program of research and development to advance cybersecurity.

In 2010, the DoD-commissioned JASON Report, Science of Cybersecurity, outlined the need to establish cybersecurity science-based centers within universities and other research institutions.[8] These Federally-funded centers would provide Government sponsors with access to the regional clusters of innovative ideas and academic experts while concurrently facilitating exposure by researchers to agency experience and expertise in managing cyber threats to Government networks. One priority should be to map the risk and potential cascading consequences associated with cyber attacks on critical physical infrastructure. A second priority should be to advance research that can support the development of technology and automated approaches to detect and mitigate attacks. And another priority should be to enrich our understanding of the human and social aspects of managing cyber vulnerabilities since advancing cyber security involves much more than technical problems.

REGIONAL UNIVERSITY-BASED CYBERSECURITY RESEARCH CENTERS

Since information and communications networks are largely owned and operated by the private sector, regional university-based cybersecurity research centers should be assigned the task of facilitating an exchange among industry, Government, and academic partners to test data and transition new ideas into the rapid adoption of research and technology development innovations. Regional university-based centers should be assigned as their primary mission, developing strategies to improve the security and resilience of information infrastructure and reducing the

---

[8] "Science of Cyber-Security" JASON, The MITRE Corp. JSR–10–102 (Nov 2010) *http://www.fas.org/irp/agency/dod/jason/cyber.pdf*.

vulnerability, mitigating the consequences, and speeding the recovery of critical infrastructure in the face of cyber attacks.

As a stepping-off point, these regional university-based research centers should be tasked with working with U.S. National research laboratories to develop a detailed profile of the physical-cyber risk to the electric grid and developing options for mitigating that risk. Understanding the technical elements of the cyber threat to the power grid is a complex, multi-disciplinary challenge, that requires an understanding of networking and protocols, software and machine architecture, formal methods and high-performance computing, nanotechnology, and quantum and compressive imaging, to name a few. Implementing potential solutions will involve an intricate array of not just technical tools, but appropriate procedural protocols, public policy, and regulations. To accomplish this task, the Department of Energy and the Department of Defense should actively support a directed research program that involves a collaborative effort amongst the U.S. National research laboratories, electric utilities, and the university-based cybersecurity research community to simulate real-life conditions, systems, and infrastructure, that would lead to the discovery, testing, and analysis of state-of-the-art tools, technologies, and software in a scientifically rigorous manner. Concurrently, the research program should identify policy guidelines and incentives for quickly integrating those tools, technologies, and software into the power grid to bolster its resilience in the face of the cyber threat. This effort should be undertaken with close collaboration with Canada given the interconnected nature of the regional grids in the East and West with the provinces of Canada.

ECONOMIC DRIVERS

Advances in networking and information technology are key economic drivers, crucial to maintaining America's global competitive position in energy and transportation, food and manufacturing, education and life-long learning, health care, and National and homeland security. If the recent past is a guide, these advances will also accelerate the pace of discovery in nearly all other fields. In the end, capitalizing on America's peerless standing in higher education by creating regional university-based centers to advance cybersecurity, will provide a rich return on investment for the Nation.

CONCLUSION

Beyond the risk of a detonation of a weapon of mass destruction on U.S. soil, no security challenge is currently more serious to the United States than the on-going risk of cyber attacks. The security of our public and private cyber networks is vital to assuring the reliability of the electric grid, transportation systems, and banking and financial systems, and consumers. Continued research collaboration with academic and industry partners is an important function for the Federal Government and vital to improving homeland security. Such partnerships provide an important return on investment as Government receives solutions tailored to its security needs, university partners employ some of their best researchers and students in an effort to develop new technologies, and the next generation of STEM professionals get the skills and training they need to enter into homeland security careers that benefit the Nation. I strongly recommend that this subcommittee direct the Department of Homeland Security to build on Secretary Napolitano's recent academic engagement efforts by more actively incorporate university partners, including establishing regional university-based cybersecurity research centers, to support the DHS's efforts to develop public-private approaches to preventing, responding, and recovering from future cyber attacks.

Thank you again for the opportunity to testify today. I would be happy to answer any questions you may have.

Mr. McCAUL. Thank you Dr. Flynn.

In fact, I offered an amendment, and Ms. Clarke was helpful with that amendment, that would basically look at these consortiums, university-based and fusion center. The bill that I introduced, that passed unanimously out of the Science and Technology Committee will be on the floor this Thursday, does create a public-private partnership between the universities and the public sector and the private sector in a task force. So I think that is a step in the right direction.

I completely agree with your analysis on that point, that universities can play such a critical role. We also have a Federal scholarship program for service in the Federal Government in that bill.

So with that, I just want to—one of the reasons we wanted to have this hearing—we have historic legislation on the floor on cybersecurity for the first time in many years, and we wanted to call to the attention of the American people and to Members of Congress as to what the real threat is. I have been dealing with this issue for a long time, but I think it is important that the American people, who most of them don't understand this issue, have a better idea of what is at risk.

You know, when I look at the theft of intellectual property to the tune of $1 trillion, that is a serious economic issue for the United States; when I look at countries like China who have stolen our Joint Strike Fighters, F–35 and F–22s, stolen those blueprints so they can manufacture those planes and then guard against those planes; when you look at China and Russia who have hacked into every Federal agency in the Federal Government, including the Pentagon.

You know, we talk about the analogy, agents of a foreign power caught with paper files walking out with classified or nonclassified information, it will be all over the papers. But yet in the virtual world, that is happening and no one seems to know or really pay attention to it.

Then the final piece. There is the espionage, the stealing of military secrets, satellite technology, rocket technology out of NASA, it is prevalent, it is everywhere; and when I look at the cyber warfare piece, that is the one that keeps me up at night the most.

As we know, the genie is out of the bottle, just like nuclear weapons. It can be turned against us. We know what our offensive capability is and it is pretty darn impressive. That capability turned against us, I think is what frightens us, and who would have the motivation to do that.

So my first question is to Mr. Henry. You said that we are really just hitting the tip of the iceberg and that the biggest threats are below the waterline. Can you expand on what these bigger threats are beneath the tip of the iceberg?

Mr. HENRY. Yes, sir. Thank you. Let me, if I could just clarify my statement that I made about the sense of urgency. I certainly recognize everything this committee is doing. My concern is the holistic response of our society, public, private, other Government agencies, and citizens themselves. So I wanted to make sure that was clear. That was my concern.

When I talk about below the iceberg, I really talk about what is being seen on the classified side. Certainly in this environment, I can't go into details. But when you have people like General Alexander from NSA, and General Hayden, former CIA and NSA, and Admiral McConnell, the Director of National Intelligence, Joel Brenner, the National Counterintelligence Executive, when you have people, they have all seen below the waterline. When they are standing up saying what they are saying, I think people need to listen to that and understand that when you have got the senior leadership of the Government talking about how significant and substantial this threat is, they have seen below the waterline, they have seen that big piece of iceberg the average person just never gets to see. What they hear about and see about in the media is really just a very small portion. I think some of the witnesses here kind of alluded to that and talked about some of the concerns about SCADA systems, industrial control systems, some of the threats to, as you mentioned, our cleared defense contractors. The threats there are so voluminous and so large and the implications—while certainly a threat of a credit card being stolen is absolutely important and I recognize that—but when you talk about the plans to our next generation weapon systems and our adversary being able to prepare a defense today or to build devices that can counter or actually exceed our capabilities, that is a significant danger to this Nation and people have to understand that.

Mr. McCAUL. When we talk about cyber Pearl Harbor, and I have the director of NSA telling me it is not a question of if but when, where do you see the biggest threat coming from?

Mr. LEWIS. I think it is two of the groups I mentioned, Mr. Chairman. I don't worry about China and Russia. They are not going to start a war just for fun. But I don't know if I would say that for Iran or North Korea when they get the capabilities. I know the full committee is going to have a hearing on Iran on Thursday, but they have a little bit of a grudge match. They feel like we are somehow responsible for Stuxnet and they are trying to create a cyber army.

The other group to watch, and the group that is more interesting that I think we have all raised, are these hacker groups who have anarchic or anti-Government tendencies, very strong cyber skills, some of them have excellent hackers involved. There are so many vulnerabilities and there are so many tools that eventually—you know, the line I always refer to is a headline we saw last year about how Anonymous declares war on Orlando, right? Well, what that meant was they defaced the Orlando City website. Maybe a year from now they will be able to do a little bit more, and I think we are on track to find that out the hard way.

Mr. McCAUL. Well, my concern with those groups is that they sometimes may be—organized crime may be the real perpetrator, but they take the credit for it and sort of provide a ruse.

I see my time is expired. I can ask a lot more questions, but thank you for being here today.

With that, I recognize the Ranking Member Mr. Keating.

Mr. KEATING. Thank you, Mr. Chairman.

Two things that were raised. The idea of incorporating protections into the design work, and another issue that was raised was the fact that you had companies that have been victims of attack and haven't been forthright in acknowledging what that is or the extent of it, what damages they had or what happened.

I think those two things call into question again the role that academia can play in this regard, being more neutral and being part of design.

With that, I would like to ask Dr. Flynn what on-going research projects are in place, not only in your university but around the country that you are aware of? How can Congress act to extend those and make that more beneficial in our efforts against cybersecurity attacks?

Mr. FLYNN. Thank you very much for your question, Ranking Member Keating. It is probably a bit overstated to say they have been missing in action, but it is not too much overstated. I mean to a large extent, we really have not engaged our academic community to work at this problem at the outset of it. Clearly we have some infrastructure in place. The Department of Homeland Security has centers of excellence that have been set up, the National Security Agency has created similar kinds of output. So you have some outreach to engage some of this enormous intellectual capital we have. But we really haven't gone into the universities and given the challenge, the kind of things that we have done in past history where we have really embraced that intellectual capital and focused it and channeled it in a constructive way.

In our area of the country up in the Northeast, in fact, five universities—Harvard, MIT, Boston University, University of Massachusetts, and my own Northeastern University—have come together with some private-sector players to build an advance cybersecurity center. Some of the folks who were in on the origin of helping to drive the information age feel some responsibility to help work it. But to the extent that kind of regional effort, we have clusters of expertise, and we have them in Texas, we have them in Seattle, we have them in big pockets across our country, the sense that we can harness that, I think through regional efforts, will be an enormously positive contribution, both to set the alarm, set the challenge, engage folks and then ultimately to work toward some solutions.

Mr. KEATING. Thank you, Dr. Flynn.

You mentioned, and Mr. McClure mentioned, that there are actual, now, transitions into physical danger; people can be murdered. I wanted to first address this to Mr. Henry and then anyone else that might want to comment on this.

But what can we do in Congress to—I am a former prosecutor myself—what can be done to extend—I would imagine the jurisdictional issues would be difficult even if you are successful in finding out who is responsible for these actions. But Mr. Henry, what can be done here in Congress to help that effort, because it will help not only bring people to justice that are responsible, but it would help as a deterrent as well. I would imagine one of the things that is difficult in this is finding a deterrent when people do this, because they might feel that they are, in a criminal sense, judgment-proof or not being able to prosecuted. So do you have any suggestions as to what we can do in Congress in that regard?

Mr. HENRY. Yes, sir. I think that you hit on it right there. With the Computer Fraud and Abuse Act primarily, we are looking at stiffening the penalties for the breaches and for those who are stealing information. I think that the deterrence is critical. I said that we have an adversary problem. These are adversaries who are launching viruses, who are launching Trojans, who are breaking into computers. There are people, and by reaching out and touching these people and taking them off the playing field, we are having an impact on the threat. It is a way for us to mitigate the threat. Stiffer penalties that are more rigorous, certainly from an enforcement perspective or an investigation perspective, I think we will have a larger impact and will raise the cost of adversaries for what they do on a day-to-day basis.

Mr. KEATING. What can we do in terms of international cooperation in this regard? Because they can be launched from any country, any jurisdiction.

Mr. HENRY. Absolutely. Anybody, anywhere in the world with an internet connection and a $500 laptop is a potential subject in any investigation. The attribution, to who may have done that type of attack, is a critical piece.

When I was in the FBI, we worked very, very closely with foreign partners. The Bureau continues to do that, as well as other agencies, where we actually put FBI agents into the National police agencies of a number of countries in Eastern Europe and Western Europe, physically sitting side by side, working these investigations. I think we have to continue that both from an intelligence-sharing perspective and from collaborative investigations.

Mr. KEATING. We have security treaties with other countries. Can you see that being expanded in terms of cybersecurity treaties with other countries around the world and expanding that to a greater level?

Mr. HENRY. I think that has got to be a constant dialogue. I mean, this is a problem that doesn't face just the United States. It faces good societies and good people around the world. People are using this as a tool and as a weapon to promote their means and to promote their criminal operations. We have to have that dialogue regularly.

Mr. KEATING. Thank you, Mr. Chairman.

Mr. McCAUL. I thank the Ranking Member. The Chairman now recognizes the Ranking Member of the full committee, Mr. Thompson, for 5 minutes.

Mr. THOMPSON. Thank you very much, Mr. Chairman. I agree with all of the comments that have been made relative to the seriousness of this issue. I listened with great interest to our panel of witnesses, and I am going to kind of ask for a little more help from you with my questions.

If you were sitting in our seat, having to craft legislation that would provide the tools that you think would be necessary to get our hands around this issue, given what you know and the seriousness of this issue, what two or three things do you think that kind of cybersecurity legislation would need? Mr. Henry, I will start with you.

Mr. HENRY. The first one, for me, that I think is the most critical is data breach reform, data breach reporting. Currently there are, as the committee knows, I am sure, 47 State data breach laws. There is a lot of confusion that I see in the private sector, from organizations that are breached, on to whom to report and when to report. I think the failure to report is a problem for all of us. I think that those companies, those infrastructures in those organizations are being used by our adversaries. They are part of the problem. If that is not reported, if there is not some type of remediation done, that continues to be a problem.

From my perspective, when I was in the FBI, in some of our most successful cases where we were able to effectively reach out across oceans and put our hands on people, it was really the times when organizations came forward very quickly, which enabled us to get attribution through analysis of their network in collaboration with them. That is really, really critical. So data breach reporting.

The second one is intelligence sharing, the ability for the Government to share broadly across infrastructure, to help raise the defenses, and to make organizations much more secure by providing some of those signatures that are not necessarily out in the hands of the general public but will enable critical infrastructure and organizations as a whole to better protect themselves.

Mr. THOMPSON. Mr. Lewis.

Mr. LEWIS. Thank you. There are some very useful bills in the House and they will do some good things. But the ultimate test will be: Do you give the Government more authority to mandate security, to protect critical infrastructure facilities? If we don't do that this year, an attack is inevitable. Now, I know that there is a lot of contention on this issue, and I know there are questions about the ability of some agencies to carry out this function. But the ultimate test will be, do we require better security for critical infrastructure? If the answer is no, the Congress will have failed.

There are good things on the information-sharing side, on the research side, but the ultimate test is critical infrastructure.

Mr. THOMPSON. Mr. Wilshusen.

Mr. WILSHUSEN. I would also echo what each of my colleagues have mentioned, but I will also talk to clearly define what the roles and responsibilities of the Federal agencies are in Federal Governments with respect to not only protecting and securing its own systems but also the support and assistance they can provide to the private sector and protecting particularly critical infrastructure sectors.

Mr. MCCLURE. I agree on the information sharing. I think it is absolutely key. But the only downside is that it is very reactive. The proactive side of it would be to really think about, how do you provide guidelines, either incentives or mandates, around secure by design? You know, a power plant might not be able to control how a PLC is designed from Germany, but they can absolutely not buy that PLC if it is not secure. So it is up to them, and I think we can provide better guidance, sir, on that.

Mr. FLYNN. Everything I have heard so far are things that I would endorse. I would certainly endorse the legislation, Mr. Chairman, you are trying to advance as well with the Ranking Member.

I would add, one of the areas that we really need to do a better job at the risk mapping; particularly across infrastructure, we have got a sector-by-sector approach. When you hit one, what we don't have is a very good understanding of how the loss of that one could impact on others. So I know the Department of Energy is looking into this. But this is something, I think with legislative support, let's map what the consequences are of these attacks. That is a great motivator for people to get into the prevention mode. I think that could be very important.

The other key area I think is, err on the side of openness. The hearing is doing, I think, a great public service. But a lot of the approach we have taken to date is work that is below the surface. You are not going to get the American people willing to invest, companies willing to invest, unless we talk about the problem with greater candor and with more specificity. I think we need to essentially err on the side of being more open about the risk to vulnerabilities, but obviously develop solutions for attacking these problems. Thank you.

Mr. THOMPSON. Thank you. I yield back, Mr. Chairman.

Mr. MCCAUL. I thank the Ranking Member.

The Chairman now recognizes the gentleman from Missouri, Mr. Long.

Mr. LONG. Thank you. Thank you all for taking your time to be here today on this important subject. I would be remiss, Dr. Flynn, if I didn't mention that for the last few months, I have had a young lady from your university, Northeastern, interning in my office. If she is emblematic of your university and of college students today, I would say that this country has a very bright future.

Mr. FLYNN. They are all exactly like her.

Mr. LONG. All righty. Send me some more, will you?

In 1941, my dad was a junior in high school. So he and people of his vintage can tell you where they were during the attack on Pearl Harbor. I can tell you where I was when JFK got assassinated. I can also tell you where—most people 16 years and older can probably tell you where they were on 9/11. We all remember that. I think I can predict with great certainty where I will be when we have our first devastating cyber attack. I have two options: I will either be in a full committee hearing on cybersecurity or a subcommittee on cybersecurity. We are good at talking things to death. It seems like we go over this again and again and again, but I have yet to really have anyone add any concrete steps that we can take to prevent such a horrific attack.

So, Mr. Lewis, if I were to ask you—I heard one a minute ago—but your top three priorities or things that we can do, take to the Congress to try to address this situation, because we keep talking it and talking it and talking it. The top three things that we can do. Just pick out three things that you think are the most vital that we can truly make an impact on this situation at preventing cyber attacks.

Mr. LEWIS. You know a lot of the legislation that is before the House and before the Senate does good stuff, but it doesn't do enough. So we have got to think about a comprehensive approach. For me, the most important step that we are not taking is thinking about how to deal with the issues of critical infrastructure vulnerability. The difference between now and, say, 5 years ago—5 years ago, it was difficult to say how to secure networks. Now I think we can tell you how to secure networks. People will not do it, though, unless——

Mr. LONG. Let me ask you—let me interrupt you for a second.

Mr. LEWIS. Sure.

Mr. LONG. Before I came to Congress I was in a business where there was a large group of people that all needed to access, from several different companies, but access the same information on the internet. We would carry a fob with us that had—I think it was a nine-digit number and that number would change about every 90 seconds. So if you wanted to log onto your computer—systems like that, would those be beneficial on a wider scale, or not?

Mr. LEWIS. Remember, what was it, last year we had a story about—it was a false story but people got all excited because they thought that Springfield, Illinois, had their water system hacked. That turned out to be not true. But the story behind it was actually a little scarier, because they weren't hacked. The contractor was calling in from Russia. I thought to myself, "That is bad in so many ways, right?" So yes, having a requirement for people to better authenticate themselves when they log into critical infrastructure networks would be a good step. There are other things we can do. But right now——

When I told you about this search software that would find vulnerabilities, the easiest vulnerability to find is—you all know when you have bought a computer, when you have bought a router, that it comes configured with the username as "administrator" and the password is "password." If you go out and look at critical infrastructure, you will find some networks have not been reconfigured. So getting people to reconfigure, getting people to better authenticate, getting people to think about what they have attached to their systems, all of these would make a big difference.

When you talk to companies and you say to them, "Do you have your control systems connected to the internet?" Almost all of them say no, right? When they say that, they believe it. Now it turns out they are always wrong, right, they don't know because these are a lot of computers. Nothing malicious here. But getting people to have a better understanding of what is connected to the internet, how it connects, and who can use it, these are all things we can do, but it won't happen magically. So that is where Congress could make a very big difference.

Mr. LONG. Okay. You were talking about Springfield, Illinois, a false story out of there.

Springfield, Missouri, my hometown. I have said this before in committee hearings. But we had a small title loan company that, over the weekend, had $440,000 removed from their account and it went to Pakistan, which we don't know if it went on to benefit al-Qaeda or what from that point.

But one real quick wrap-up question for Mr. Henry: Why am I concerned if it is China, Russia, Iran, why do I care where these attacks come from? Don't we need to be concerned with combating the problem more than where it is coming from? Everybody goes back to where it might be coming from.

Mr. HENRY. Well, sir, I think that it is really important for us to understand who the adversary is so we can take other actions. I say that we have an adversary problem. I think there are things we can do as a Government to define for the adversaries what the red lines are and what the repercussions are for crossing those red lines. So if in fact we were able to identify that a particular country took the plans to our next-generation fighter plane, that we would take actions, as a country, against them, whatever it may be, whether it be diplomatic, economic, or military.

Mr. LONG. But to prevent that from happening the next time——

Mr. HENRY. So from my perspective, I think if we, as people who are monitoring security on networks, have an understanding of who the adversary is, the tactics, techniques, procedures that they are using, the information that they are going after, we can get a better sight picture of who that adversary is, and it helps us to better defend. It helps us from a strategic perspective.

If you are protecting the network and you know a particular country is looking for plans to a particular device, you can change how that data is stored, you can change how it is transmitted, you can change how it is maintained on the network. There are actually procedures that network owners can take to better defend themselves.

So I believe that using intelligence and by being proactive, you can be predictive and then preventive. You can predict who is going to attack what and where, and it helps you prevent.

Mr. LONG. I am way past my time. I yield back.

Mr. MCCAUL. I thank the gentleman.

Just on the point of specific recommendations, I wanted to brag on my colleague, Mr. Lewis. The CSIS report made many specific recommendations. Some have been taken up by the Congress and some have not, but I want to thank you again for that great work.

With that, I recognize the gentlelady from New York, Ms. Clarke.

Ms. CLARKE. Thank you very much Mr. Chairman. I thank our Ranking Member for this very important Oversight, Investigations, and Management Subcommittee hearing. I want to associate my comments with the comments of Mr. Long about frustration when it comes to to this conversation about the urgent action that is required to protect our Nation's infrastructure from the constant barrage and bombardment, the attack on our systems, because it just seems as though we just keep having this conversation. Understanding the threat that we are under, understanding the constant attack that we are under, but we are not making the types of headway that we need to make.

All of us have a role to play here. We have a legislative role to play. It seems that we tinker at the margins. I am very concerned that—you know, as a New Yorker, someone who could not have imagined that airplanes could be turned into missiles, that we are not imagining the real devastation that we could be under with the click of a mouse at any point in time. So, gentlemen, I think—you know your expertise is well noted.

One of the things that I would like to ask of you is whether you have had an opportunity to review the bill that was passed out of the Homeland Security Committee for cybersecurity and whether any of you are in a position to comment on that legislation?

This is Cybersecurity Week. There are a number of bills that are moving to the floor to be passed this week, but none of which have the level of comprehensiveness as the bill that was passed out of this committee; yet that won't be taken up this week. So I am just trying to figure out how serious we are here and what each of you respectively believes should be the next move of this legislative body when it comes to legislation.

Don't all click at once. I don't want to put anyone on the spot. Some folks may not have had an opportunity to see it yet. But Mr. Lewis, you are nodding so maybe you can——

Mr. LEWIS. Yes. I think I am the stuck key on this one initially. The original bill that emerged from the committee I think was a very strong bill and would have gone a long way to putting us in a better position than we are today. I think a lot of people were

surprised when we saw the amendment. The easiest way to describe it is the original bill was, I believe, 45 pages and the amend-
ed bill was 34 pages. So the question you want to ask is: What was
in those 11 pages that came out? If I had any advice, it might be
to add those 11 pages back in. These are always difficult issues.

If I have learned one lesson this year, it is that you shouldn't try
to do major legislation in an election year. But I think this is a case
where we can put the two bills side by side and see one—and I applaud the authors of it—one was very strong. The other is less
strong. So maybe we need to reconsider.

Mr. McCLURE. I am not detailed around some of the bills that
have come up. But I will say that we have always found that incentives tend to motivate quite a bit, but they have to be specific. Anything around, for example, finding the problem before a bad guy
does or finding the vulnerabilities, for example, and then patching
and fixing them in an acceptable window of time, what we call the
window of exposure, right?

We are also enforcing, as we talked about earlier, enforcing
strong authentication. It is really hitting—if you can just hit the
80/20 rule of security, which is that 80 percent of the risk is rep-
resented by 20 percent of the problems, you are going to go a long,
long way to making it simple to do, but also very impactful.

Mr. FLYNN. If I might just add, clearly one of the core issues has
been, to what extent should Government play a more enforcement
role. Clearly one of the issues that we have seen laid out here is
the market has not been able unto itself to figure out how to put
together adequate standards that are essentially being enforced
within the market to deal with this risk. What has been particularly a problem is information providers interacting with critical infrastructure owners, people in the physical world who often are un-
aware of the vulnerabilities that they are investing in.

There is a moral hazard problem there. We typically deal with
moral hazard through some form of standard-setting and enforcement of that standard. The bottom line here is that this is an interesting philosophical battle. But at a practical level, we need a much
more mature process for identifying standards and figuring out
how to enforce them. So where I think we should be more creative
is around third parties as a fee-based approach, whatever is required here. But at the end of the day, purely voluntary approaches
I think will not get us to where we need to be.

Ms. CLARKE. Thank you, Mr. Chairman. I yield back.

Mr. McCAUL. Thank you. The Chairman now recognizes the gentleman from South Carolina, Mr. Duncan.

Mr. DUNCAN. Thank you, Mr. Chairman. Just a quick question:
If Congressman Long sent a tweet out during a hearing on cybersecurity, is that a contradiction?

I just got a Facebook message from someone that said, "Please
vote 'no' on SISA, SOPA, PIPA, and H.R. 1981."

There is dramatic concern within the populace that there will be
a Government overreach as we try to protect American systems on
the private sector and the public sector. So I think we have got to
tread lightly. What has been a concern of mine is: Where do we
cross the line as a Government trying to protect our citizens when
it comes to civil liberties and private information that will be not

only captured during this process but possibly retained? We had a long debate about retention of that and when it should be eradicated from the computer files. But is it ever really eradicated? There are a lot of questions that came to mind during that debate that I think are definitely worthy of further discussion, especially this week.

But Mr. McClure, I have got a question for you: What is the role of the public sector in protecting the United States Government institutional systems and the role of the private sector, primarily the free market, which I firmly believe that the free market can do it better than any Government entity?

A case in point would have been Cash for Clunkers. If a private entity would have been running that program, I don't think we would have seen the problems that we saw from the dealers.

So primarily the free market, in finding solutions to protect American systems, both public and private. So where is that balance? From the Federal Government, the public sector, trying to protect its institutions and also raise awareness of this, but the private sector and the free market finding those solutions for us.

Mr. MCCLURE. Well, I think that when it comes to the private sector, obviously the buck is what motivates, right? So if they can either sell more stuff, more products, more widgets, because it is secure or because it is more secure than a competitor, that draws a lot of interest. So from an incentive perspective, that works out quite well.

I think when you start to move to the public sector, there is little incentive around that of making an extra buck. So from that perspective, I think you know more mandates and more guidelines have to be enforced. Now, where the two come together, in my book, is they really haven't, up until this point, and they need to in some form or fashion bring together both sides at the top levels to—not just for information sharing but also for helping to set and establish the guidelines that each other will be measured against, if you will, around security. Because this is very—it is actually quite simple to prevent a lot of bad stuff from happening that is just not happening. That has been the frustration in doing this for 20-plus years, is we know what solves this problem. It is just an issue of getting people to move and act to do it, and making it a priority within their organization. That is the bottom line.

Mr. DUNCAN. I know academia is working with both. So I am going to ask you to step out of that and ask—we have got some public entities there. Do y'all want to answer that question? Do you want to chime in on that?

Mr. LEWIS. Well, two points: It is a good question. The first is knowing the work that Chairman Rogers and Ranking Member Ruppersberger have done on the bill. It is not SOPA, right? There is an effort to try to tag SOPA to it because everyone hates SOPA and they go ballistic when they hear it.

They have made an effort to protect privacy. I think the changes in that bill are essential. You know, they update old legislation from the 1980s, from dial phones and copper wires, to let Government and companies work together better. So when I look at the bill, I don't think it poses a great risk to privacy. I realize there are concerns. Perhaps when it goes to conference or when it moves along in the voting process, those can be addressed.

Mr. DUNCAN. Thank you, Mr. Chairman. I don't have anything further. I yield back.

Mr. MCCAUL. Thank you. The Chairman now recognizes the gentleman from Illinois, Mr. Davis.

Mr. DAVIS. Thank you very much, Mr. Chairman. Thank you, gentlemen, very much for being here.

I guess we have always been concerned about the economic impact and never have we been more concerned about it than now. I often hear people try to estimate, say, what the cost of security operations are, what the impact of 9/11 has been on our economy, and what the economy would be like perhaps if we had not experienced that attack, and all of the different things that we have had to do to try to prevent it from occurring.

There are estimates and studies that have suggested that there might be as much of an annual cost of about $40 billion a year from cyber attacks. Do any of us know how that information was arrived at, or the basis upon which those estimates are being made?

Mr. WILSHUSEN. I would just say from our view, we don't know exactly how that information has been derived or the methodology. Indeed, in many cases we have found that cyber crime is often underreported and the amounts and estimates that are made, they vary widely from, you know, tens of billions to hundreds of billions. So the actual amount that has been the result of cyber crime, it is hard to really difficult. But it is likely to be a very large number.

Mr. LEWIS. If I could just add to that. I used to think that people just used a magic eight ball and if they didn't like the number, they flipped it. But there are a couple of things we can look at.

The first is I would note that the National Intelligence Council is attempting to estimate the cost of cyber losses. The Economic Intelligence Unit, which is a branch of the *Economist* magazine is doing it. Cambridge University is doing an estimate. So in the next year, we might see three estimates.

One thing you could look at is you could look at Germany which did its own estimate of its losses through cyber espionage, economic espionage. I believe the figure they came up with was about $24 billion. Now the U.S. economy is five times as large as the German economy, so that gives you a range. We don't have a good figure, but we are working on it. It looks to me like it will be in the low hundreds of billions.

Mr. FLYNN. I was just going to add, Congressman, that I think you made a very compelling analogy. The cost often is what happens after a catastrophic event. So when we have a cyber Pearl Harbor, that is where we really start to see the numbers, in part because of the rush to deal with the uncertainty.

The case I try to make to my private-sector friends when we talk about these issues, we are, No. 1, trying to prevent things, but we are also trying to prevent the overreaction, the associated cost. That is why getting standards at the outset, agreed upon, that pass the smile test, those are critical in terms of protecting our economy, protecting the market against these kinds of threats.

Mr. DAVIS. There are some people who think that we might be engaged in a bit of overkill in terms of how much time, energy, effort, money, everything else that we are putting into the notion of trying to create as secure an environment as we can possibly have. What would you say to people who express that kind of thought?

Mr. MCCLURE. I would say that it is a little shortsighted, that it is as big as you hear, and probably three to four times. I have done countless, hundreds and hundreds of investigations, incident response exercises, and have cleaned up after. I can tell you that the estimates that have come from all those engagements are typically far diluted because of their—No. 1, just inability to actually quantify the loss. The attempts to do it are quite flawed, especially because of the urgency of the remediation attempts. So for me, it is highly underestimated.

Mr. DAVIS. So you would still say the old adage that an ounce of prevention is worth much more than a pound of cure?

Mr. MCCLURE. Without a doubt.

Mr. DAVIS. Thank you, gentlemen, very much. Thank you, Mr. Chairman. I yield back.

Mr. MCCAUL. I thank the gentleman. Let me just in closing say, first of all, thank you for being here. You provide great insight.

We do have four bills going forward this week. With respect to the bill that passed out of this committee, I do believe it has the core components that the Secretary and the director of NSA asked for, and that is codification of existing legal authorities and an information-sharing system through the National Cybersecurity and Communications Integrations Center. We also have the ISECS out there as well.

I know the intel bill also makes DHS a hub for cyber threat information sharing within the Government. I think anytime we deal with the private sector, we always have to be careful of that balance of incentivizing versus unduly burdensome mandates. It is always a balance between security and that. I would always prefer to incentivize when possible. But this is a very, very important, serious issue. And it is my sincere hope, as I mentioned to the Ranking Member of the full committee—you being Ranking on the cybersecurity committee—that we can work together on this important legislation. The issue is too important for the American people. I think everybody standing up here or sitting here at the dais understands that.

So with that, we thank the witnesses again. Without objection, this hearing is adjourned.

[Whereupon, at 3:35 p.m., the subcommittee was adjourned.]

APPENDIX

STATEMENT OF JOHN WATTERS, CHAIRMAN AND CEO, iSIGHT PARTNERS, INC.

APRIL 24, 2012

Chairman McCaul, Vice Chairman Long, Ranking Member Keating, and other distinguished Members of the subcommittee, thank you for the opportunity to offer testimony to the Subcommittee on Oversight, Investigations, and Management.

My name is John Watters and I am the Founder, Chairman, and CEO of iSIGHT Partners, Inc, a highly-specialized cyber risk management company. We launched over 5 years ago to help the public and private sectors assess and adapt their security measures against the rapidly intensifying cyber threat environment. The insights we provide into adversarial capability drives efficient resource utilization and focus on key threat concerns as opposed to noise that cannot be translated into mitigation. At our core, iSIGHT Partners has a world-class cyber threat intelligence capability delivering research, analysis, and a "community defense" against emerging threats from around the globe.

Threats to the cyber environment where our citizens, critical infrastructure, industry, and governments operate have intensified dramatically in recent years. This should come as no surprise, as the efficiency, effectiveness, and anonymity of cyber attacks have expanded to encompass every traditional threat category. Criminals understand that stealing no longer requires putting themselves in danger by committing traditional crimes using a weapon, such as bank robbery. In today's high-tech world, criminals easily and efficiently steal millions of dollars simply by creating aliases and obtaining a few keystrokes from their victims using tools readily available in underground forums. Nationalist actors recognize that they need not risk human assets to gain access to vital National interests when they can navigate the connected world of computers to establish a virtual presence and route information back home without a passport or visa and without leaving an evidentiary trail. The shift from the physical space to cyber space has already transpired, and the resulting risks to industries and governments are substantial and growing. Unfortunately, we continue to look internally for ways to combat cyber crime, when the solution requires that we look externally.

Given the incredibly complex set of challenges we face in securely and efficiently managing our businesses and the Government while contending with these increased risks, we must embrace change as a constant and adapt accordingly. Absent an adaptive defense to an adaptive threat environment, we will fall further behind in our ability to prevent successful attacks targeting our interests. And small businesses, as the innovation engine of our country, are able to focus on not only confronting but actually outstripping the adversary's rapid pace.

In the past, in what could now be called "Cybersecurity 1.0," we resourced internal environments with a layered approach of people, processes, and technologies. This approach began at the perimeter and layered back to the core, where critical operations and information reside. However, as technologies have become more advanced and interconnected, these layers have shrunk, and the adversary's ability to traverse our networks has grown tremendously. In some cases, this phenomenon relates to bad security practices, such as password reuse. In other ways, the complexity of our own environments increases likely ingress and attack points through which adversaries can gain access to our critical information. While our defenses are enhanced because we can correlate events from different devices in different layers, the reality is that our adversaries have watched our slow adaptation and responded accordingly with more sophisticated and coordinated attacks; they are adapting to our moves, but we are slow to comprehend and adapt to theirs.

However, improvements to our cybersecurity posture should not go unnoticed. Now that we have resourced our environment and refined our overall security posture, our future success in combating cyber threats resides in our ability to tactically and operationally adapt our defense to new and emerging attack methodologies. We now have a security infrastructure that we can manage, but the question is whether we manage it with insight into our adversaries and their capabilities or continue to blindly attempt to secure critical intellectual property and information. In summary, "Cybersecurity 1.0" was vulnerability-based, and we benchmarked ourselves against regulations and what we thought were best practices. However, absent adversary insight, we will continue to hunt in our own environment for vulnerabilities that, in many cases, have already been exploited and try to close those security gaps. We have taken this approach for more than a decade with very little success. To more effectively combat cybercrime, we must move away from the old model and begin to benchmark our countermeasure posture in light of current attacks executed within our borders and from abroad and adapt our defenses accordingly.

Now we need to exceed the innovation pace of our adversaries. As our country's global advantage has traditionally centered on the creativity spawned by small businesses, it is imperative we feed this innovation engine and embrace industry advances in this mission. Consequently, "Cybersecurity 2.0" must better manage our environment in light of the adversary's capabilities and attack methods and defend against the "new normal" of increased threat pace and capabilities. Addressing how to effectively manage decentralized environments associated with National infrastructure, global businesses and globally distributed networks where our sensitive data, processes, and intellectual property reside is the challenge. We need to decentralize our awareness outward beyond our perimeter. Rather than focus on what we alone see, our goal should be to build a common shared understanding of the threats we face with a focus on knowledge rather than more data. Just as important, we need to learn from each other's experiences. The key message is that one entity's reactive can be the next entity's proactive if these insights are rapidly shared. In others words, where we have common concerns and common threats with which to contend, we need common insights with shared solutions to combat those shared problems. Given the broad range of motivations behind adversaries using very similar attack methods, sharing individual lessons learned to create a "community defense" will enable businesses and Government to more effectively combat cyber crime.

The strategy of volunteer coordination or using a variety of Government entities for sharing is riddled with challenges. For example, one of the more critical challenges facing the traditional intelligence mission lies in the classification structure that renders real-time information sharing across common stakeholders—most managing unclassified networks—unfeasible. These security restrictions essentially prevent cyber threat intelligence analysis from being shared. In other words, most of the intelligence sourcing from the Federal sector takes place in secure environments, and the resulting analysis of attacks is inherently difficult to share.

In addition, the current construct of information sharing is limited by the absence of a trusted intermediary that can convert shared information into actionable intelligence and rapidly deliver that intelligence to each community member. To convert this idea into action and enable entities to proactively support the entire community, each community member must help fund tactical, operational, and strategic intelligence information gathering.

We need a global window into and network of all research resources. Federal security activities tend to focus deeply on a relatively tight set of specific cyber threats. However, global commercial entities do not have that luxury because their people, information, and networks are globally distributed. Therefore, they must gain access to emerging threat data and victim data from around the world, rather than from one specific nation, sector, or entity. This requires community-building around the world, developing relationships and focusing on the transfer of knowledge rather than simply deploying machine sensors that witness technical indicators and events. Without the context associated with the indicators, it is impossible to attribute an attack to the appropriate threat category and source data that is associated with the analysis. Absent context, community members cannot effectively assess whether they are seeing something of critical importance or just another spam attack.

In summary, we need an analytical pace that matches the rapidly developing pace of cyber threats. This is a resource- and time-intensive activity requiring complete integration of global insight, an analytical team and structure that processes information into structured analytical products and a delivery method that enables community members to filter analysis based on the appropriate and specific customer and operation. An executive in one department of the Federal Government has a very different set of needs from a security operations center analyst in a fusion center, which is different from the fraud prevention team of an on-line bank with branches in Europe and South America. In short, intelligence analysis must address tactical, operational, and strategic needs while supplying various views of the analysis for each community member's category and sector.

Since June 1, 2010, iSIGHT Partners has been fortunate to provide these capabilities in support of the entire Federal, State, and local civilian government through a single enterprise contract with the Department of Homeland Security's (DHS) United States Computer Emergency Readiness Team (US–CERT). Over the past 9 months alone, iSIGHT Partners has delivered more than 18,000 intelligence reports and updates with more than 8,500 associated technical threat indicators. During the same 9-month period, we responded to nearly 500 analysis requests while holding nearly 200 meetings with those we support. Most recently, US–CERT has begun leveraging a large number of our indicators as part of its Joint Cybersecurity Services Pilot. These threat indicators connect to specific intelligence analyses which enable each unique organization to tune their own security environment to detect and defend against specific cyber attacks that have been observed and analyzed. As threat indicators are triggered, defenders now have context about what attack was just defeated based on its connection to associated analysis. To that end, for example, Section 935 of the Ike Skelton National Defense Authorization Act for Fiscal Year 2011 established the requirement for progress reports from the Department of Defense requiring just this sort of shift toward contextual knowledge. And as many of our Government users have recognized, this is a game-changer for Government security operations. Enabling context and threat categorization in real time also enables defenders to prioritize resources and focus on serious cyber threats rather than taking the traditional approach of attempting to deal with all attacks equally.

This contracting approach demonstrates the forward-leaning, innovative leadership within US–CERT and DHS. In today's budget climate, and as recognized by the current administration's Federal Information Technology Shared Services Strategy paradigm of "Shared First," common problems must be addressed with common solutions. The ability to contract and deliver this shared solution across the mission space is a case study illustrating that fact. Through this program, visibility into global cyber attacks against commercial and Government entities has improved tremendously. Together with US–CERT, iSIGHT Partners has driven a public-private partnership, an operational level of information sharing, a mechanism to detect and defeat emerging cyber attacks while learning from other community experiences and maintained the integrity of non-classified cyber threat intelligence shared unconstrained among Federal, State, and local civilian government members. This approach has provided insight into each member's cyber defense experiences without disclosing an individual victim's identity—this is what "community defense" is all about.

Change in the cyber threat environment will be constant, and the cyber adversaries our country faces are excellent at sharing information and learning from each other's experiences. While we have made some progress in sharing information through coordination centers, in order to surpass the innovation pace of our adversaries, entrepreneurial companies like iSIGHT Partners have demonstrated a clear capability to embrace this reality. In the end, if we do not shift to an adaptive defense based on continuously updated, actionable, and sharable threat intelligence, our National interests will remain at great risk.

Thank you again for this opportunity to testify. Most importantly, I want to thank each of you for your contributions to the country and your leadership in working what is quickly emerging as one of the most important challenges facing the United States.

○